the magic if

Elizabeth Y. Kelly

the magic if

Stanislavski for Children

Photography by David W. Gifford.   Drawings by Gretchen Kelly.

NATIONAL EDUCATIONAL PRESS • Baltimore, Maryland

First Edition

International Standard Book Number: 0-87071-007-1
Library of Congress Catalog Card Number: 72-88237

National Educational Press
711 St. Paul Street
Baltimore, Maryland 21202

Printed In the United States of America

"Imagination is more important than knowledge."
Albert Einstein

This book is dedicated to the memory of
Konstantin Stanislavski and Nemirovich Dantchenko
— whose work in the Moscow Art Theatre enabled
actors everywhere to find more truth in their make
believe.

Contents

Hello, Kids   i

Dear Student   v

A Note to the Parent or Teacher   vii

1. What is the Stanislavski System?   1
2. "The Magic If"   9
3. Awareness and Imagination   19
4. Concentration: Circles of Attention   31
5. Using Your Five Senses   37
6. Extending Your Senses: Voice   43
7. The Memory of Feelings   53
8. Truth on the Stage   63
9. Communication and Communion   73
10. Adaptation   87
11. Pacing Your Role with Tempo and Rhythm   95
12. Discovering Meaning Through Actions   101
13. The Super-Objective (Main Idea) and the Through Line of Action (Lifeline)   109
14. The "Watcher Within"   117
15. Creating the Character   127
16. More Work on the Part   139

Parent/Teacher Guide: Notes on Exercises and Practice Projects   147

Parent/Teacher Guide: Exercises and Practice Projects   153

Hello, Kids,

The lady who wrote this book asked me to do an introduction for it, telling you a little bit about what's in it and what I think of it. Since it would help you to know who I am, I'll take a second to fill you in. I've acted in quite a few plays and musicals on Broadway, and I've made three or four movies and thousands of television shows. I also happen to like kids.

Writing a book to tell young people about old man Stanislavski and his method of acting is one of those wonderful ideas that makes you say, as people probably did when the band-aid got invented, "Why didn't somebody think of that before?" The method is right for kids and kids are right for the method. Children are natural actors. They learn just about everything . . . walking, talking, (lying) . . . by imitating grown-ups and "acting" like them. When little kids play "house," they start to talk, look and move like moms and dads. When a kid points his finger at another kid and says "Bang, you're dead," he means it and feels it — he's acting. The only difference between play-acting and acting in front of an audience is that when you're in front of an audience, you know people are watching you (like your mom and dad and your friends) — and you can't help thinking about it, as well as about your part.

Now it's a fact about the mind that it can't be in two places at once; it can only think of one thing at a time. Try it and you'll see! Think about

i

something in the room you're in . . . a chair or a lamp, and then think of something outside . . . a dog or a car. You'll see that you can't think of both things at once. Even if you make your mind race back and forth . . . for the split second you're thinking of the chair, you can't think about the dog, and vice-versa.

The main thing that makes someone a bad actor is stage fright. Stage fright happens when an actor (a kid in a school play or a big star on Broadway) suddenly in spite of himself thinks "They're all out there looking at me; I'd better be good." The minute he thinks that . . . the minute his mind zeroes in on the people "out front," he stops thinking "I am The King" (or whatever part he's playing), and he starts thinking "I am poor Joe Jerk, the actor, up here in front of all these people who probably aren't going to like me." Then, the prediction is apt to come true.

The purpose of "the method" is to find ways to make yourself think "I am The King." Then, because your mind can't think of more than one thing at a time, it won't be able to wonder about the people in the audience and whether they like you. The show will go on, and you'll be so busy thinking about yourself as "The King" that when it comes time to take a bow at the end, you'll be surprised to hear the applause and realize it's you they're clapping for.

It's a rule of life that if we try too hard for something, we don't get it. If a guy's out swimming in a lake and he gets a cramp and is afraid he's going to drown, he's better off not waving his arms around like crazy, trying to save himself. If he does, he'll swallow a lot of water and sink. But if he relaxes and does nothing, he'll float, and probably the cramp will go away. Anyway, he'll have a chance to get rescued. To put it another way, if a kid wants to be liked too much, if he wears a fake smile on his face all the time and "comes on too strong," the other kids are apt not to like him . . . they get turned off. But if a kid doesn't care that much about whether he's liked, if he just goes about his business and does the things he's interested in, other kids are apt to be drawn to him and like him. The Stanislavski method is a way of teaching actors not to want to be liked too much . . . not to think about it, but to go about the business of making believe they're the characters they're supposed to be.

Stanislavski lived in Russia in the old days, and he was the director of something called the Moscow Art Theater. He didn't invent "the method," he collected it. He went around talking to all of the really good actors in the world, trying to find out what it was that made them better than the others. He asked them how they acted . . . what they did to make themselves feel like, look like and act like the part they were supposed to be. He made notes of what they told him and when he got home and read the notes over, he found out that all good actors work the same way. (At least, they do a lot of stuff the same. It comes out differently, because no two people are alike.) So he made a list of the things good actors do and the order they do them in, when they're getting ready to play a part . . . and he called it a method of acting. He wrote books about it and taught it to the actors in his theater in Moscow . . . and it's come to be known as the Stanislavski method, even though it's really the method that good actors have always used anyway, which Stanislavski just bothered to find out about. (It's a little like America being named after Americus Vespucci, the mapmaker. He didn't invent America or even discover it, but he did put information about it down on paper so other people could understand it.)

It's really fun to be in a school play; and the things Mrs. Kelly has put in this book will make it even more fun, because it feels good to do things well. A few of you may decide to go on and become professional actors. If so, you'll have a head-start by having learned the things all good professionals have to learn sooner or later anyway. If you just have the fun of being an amateur actor, the things you'll learn from the method will help you to feel more sure of yourselves and to understand characters (people) and how they "act" (and why).

One word of warning: don't take any method of doing things too seriously. Acting is hard work but it's also fun. If it isn't fun for the actor, it isn't fun for the audience. You should work hard at the things Mrs. Kelly suggests, to prepare for your part; but when you're on stage, you should forget it all and let what happens happen. Your work will pay off; you'll find yourself thinking about the character instead of wondering "Do they like me?" But you'll also be enjoying yourself, which is after all the whole point.

Have fun!
Orson Bean

Dear Student:

The Magic If is your book. It was written for you alone. The chapters are directed to you, the student. Your teacher or parent will work with you on the *Exercises* in class or at home and you, yourself, will then prepare the groundwork for the next session by doing the *Practice Projects* on your own.

So there are really three of us working together: (1) I am giving you the ideas and inspirations of Stanislavski, the originator of this system of acting; (2) You are reading, absorbing and working with this material; and (3) Your parent or teacher is standing by as your director to check out your work and see that your efforts have been fruitful.

A director stands in for the audience. He listens to the actors in the play with the ears of an audience and is therefore able to tell the actor whether or not he (as audience) was affected by the performance in the desired way or if some oversight of the actor has left him unmoved. So listen to your director (parent/teacher) and be ready to grow and gain by his reactions to your performance. It is this "communication" between you that will show you the way to success as an actor.

You are lucky because you have a parent/teacher who has consented to become your own, private audience at the *preview* of your public performances. You are lucky too because you must receive a bonus when you do this enjoyable work. Your bonus will be nothing less than added pleasure and confidence in your everyday life. When you have studied the Stanislavski system, you will have a "horn of plenty" — for with every exercise you add to your experience of life, and each addition multiplies itself a hundredfold as you practice the art of living more completely.

Don't be afraid to take your MAGIC IF out of the classroom and into the wider world of life. In that way you will grow not only as an actor but, more important, as a person. It will help in all your being and becoming.

Good luck,
Elizabeth Y. Kelly

A Note to the Parent or Teacher:

As you will see when you work with this book, the basic idea behind the Stanislavski system of acting is really the heightened appreciation of life and living. Once the student has mastered the use of his five senses, he can go on to interpret what he sees, feels, hears, tastes and smells to an audience. The essential thing, however, is to open the doors of the senses wide . . . and to give the child a chance to use them fully so that when he does appear onstage (in a school production for instance), he will have extrasensory perception of a sort. He will have his sensory nerves tuned up to a higher pitch — one from which he can reach out with his new perception to touch the hearts and minds of his audience.

Even if you do not expect your child ever to appear in a play or skit, he will have had an opportunity, through the study of this system, to use his senses to the fullest extent of his capabilities. If he spends some time on these Exercises, you will be astonished at the rate and quality of his personal growth. I have used this material both with my own youngsters and in drama classes I have taught, and the results in personality growth of my pupils were a tribute to the insights of Stanislavski. Teachers will find the student develops a much greater all-around potential beyond the specific ability to perform convincingly before an audience.

Working together, you — the Parent or Teacher — will be the director, and your child will be the actor, preparing work to perform for you. Help him all you can — you must be at once audience and critic of his performances in these Exercises. If he is getting himself across to you, you may be assured he will reach the wider audience of classroom or assembly hall when he does have a part to perform in a school play.

Aside, from the **Parent/Teacher Guide:** *Notes on Exercises and Practice Projects*, which you will find in a separate section beginning on page 153, this book is directed to the pupil himself. Thus the child can practice some of these exercises at home, by himself, to prepare for the following lesson without further interpretation being necessary on your part. I want to keep it flexible, however, so that whenever the teacher or parent feels the need to "step in" and help or interpret, he may — without reservations.

One additional note: Chapter Three — on awareness and imagination — is one of the longest in the book. It seemed to me important to spend more time on developing these means to the ends the rest of the book envisions.

STAND UP. Don't just stand. . . .
stand for a purpose.
Make us see
what that purpose is.

SIT. Think before you begin.
Why are you sitting
in this scene?

1. What *Is* the Stanislavski System?

What is your favorite TV program? Why do you like it? Which character moves you the most — makes you laugh or cry?

What this book is going to do for you who work with it is to help you discover what makes that program and that actor or actress tick. Together, we shall discover what it is an ordinary person must have in order to turn himself or herself into an entirely new and different character — if only for half an hour when you are watching him or her on your favorite program. We shall look into some methods of preparation for the actor's role and see how they can lead him to a better performance. When we know how this is done well, we will have taken the first step in learning how to *act* ourselves.

The things I am going to show you were discovered many years ago by actors and actresses on the stage. Finally the whole system of study — exercises and special methods of *changing*, as if by magic, from yourself into an entirely new human being — was written down. Several books were published about this system by a Russian actor and director named Konstantin Stanislavski — thus the system was named after the man who worked with it all his life. It has been used successfully by actors of stage, screen and television for years. It can be used successfully by you, in interpreting or portraying characters in your own class plays. It is really quite a simple method and can be used by anyone who is willing to take a little time and effort to learn it. It is simply a way of looking at everything a little more closely, listening to everything a little more attentively and really *appreciating* more the colors, the feel and texture of our world. When we do this first, then we can interpret these things for an audience. But in the meantime, we also interpret them with more clarity or understanding for ourselves.

What we'll be doing in the next few chapters will be helping ourselves as actors to understand our craft so that if we want to, we may eventually put on a skit or play. We will also be beginning again to use our five senses to help us gain a new understanding of our world, starting right here at home and at school. In the first six lessons we will spend our time on some things to sharpen us up, to make us see and hear and feel — before we even try to read any parts in plays. We shall prepare ourselves just as some famous actors have done before us. We're going to see what it is that can change an ordinary person into that famous TV star you liked so much . . . and we'll begin right now with *bodily action.*

If you will think of your bodily action in these Exercises rather than your feelings, this will help you to relax and perform better. Always be specific (that is to say, be *definite* and *particular*) — do not think in generalities. You are a *specific* person in a *specific* situation. You are not people, generally. If you try to remember that, it will help make your action truthful and clear to the audience.

Exercise I. *Bodily Actions* (Teacher or parent: Please see Guide beginning on page 147.)

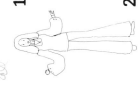

1. **Stand up.** Don't just stand — stand for a purpose. Give everything a meaning. For instance, stand to have your head above water (tread water) in a swimming pool. Stand to see better from the back row at a ball game. Think first of what your surroundings are; when you can see them, then make us see.

2. **Walk.** Give it a purpose. Walk while you are waiting for someone. Walk toward your classroom where you are about to have a test. Show us — by your attitude, your facial expression, the way you move your body — how you feel in each instance. Think before you begin. Is your friend late? Are you impatient? Think: Are you prepared for the test or afraid to take it?

3. **Sit down.** Sit because you are tired. You have just come in from a long walk. Sit in a waiting room. Think before you begin. Are you tired because you walked so far? Will you take your shoes off to rest your feet better? Think: Are you in the anteroom of the principal's office wondering why you have been called there? Will he praise you for something well done or accuse you for some wrongdoing? How do you feel about it? Are you nervous? Or is it a routine matter about which you have been informed — and are now eager to get over with? Do you wish he would hurry and see

you so you can get back to something else you were doing? In each case your reaction should be different. Let us see the action.

4. **Clean out your dresser drawer.** How will you do this? Take the whole drawer to your bed and sit next to it? Stand over the opened drawer removing articles and placing them on top of the dresser? Sit down on the floor with the drawer beside you? Think before you begin. How do you do it normally? As you take the things out, hold and examine them so that we may see with you whether you are holding a pair of socks or a shirt, a piece of jewelry or a baseball, a diary or a comic book. What do you keep in your drawers? Have you a wastebasket handy to discard broken or unwanted things? Let us see what you are doing. Structure everything and give the items shape in your hands.

5. **Run.** Run for exercise in the schoolyard. Run because someone is chasing you and you are afraid. First think: Which time would you be smiling? Think how you feel when you are afraid. Now show us the *action*.

6. **Jump.** Jump up to see over the others' heads at a parade. Jump because you are playing a game. Jump from one stone to another as you cross a brook.

Exercise I.

Structure each jump according to the story behind it. Think what you are doing, and then let us see your action.

Practice Project. Before you begin the next chapter, I want to give you some work to prepare for it at home. You will find these *Practice Projects* in each chapter. You must do the "research work" yourself and be ready to show the results at your next session with teacher or parent.

Between now and your next meeting with parent or teacher, then, I want you to do one simple thing. Pick out one person — it may be anyone you wish — from your mother to your baby brother to one of your teachers at school. It may be a friend or even a neighbor or a person you see frequently in your neighborhood. When you have selected your subject. all you have to do is to pay attention to him or her. Whenever you see this person, I want you to listen, first of all, to the voice. How does he speak? Slowly? Does he sound tired? Sincere? Does he try to make what he says seem funny? Does he talk so fast you can scarcely understand all he says? Does he have an accent?

First, then, *listen. Next, look.* Take a good look at him. Is he fat? Thin? Medium? Tall? Short? How about his posture? Does he stand straight or stooped over because he feels too tall and tries to minimize his height? Does he stoop because he's tired? *Listen and look.* And before you begin the next chapter, I want you to tell your teacher or parent just what you found out about this person that you hadn't known (or hadn't *noticed*) before. You may make

Practice Project

notes, or if you have a good memory, take mental notes. I don't care which way you do it, but be able to tell all that you have observed at the next meeting with your teacher or parent. If you are using this book at school, you may choose to portray one of your classmates. Perhaps your teacher will allow the class to guess who it is after you have fully described the person of your choice. You may tell *about* that person or you may *act him out* for the rest of the class: walking, sitting, standing and talking in the manner of the person you have observed.

I hope you have enjoyed your work up to now. In our next chapter we shall talk about the MAGIC IF.

What
would you
do IF . . .

. . .you suddenly
realized you were
on the wrong bus?

2. "The Magic If"...

On the stage we play a wonderful game of *pretend*. We pretend actually *to be* the character we are portraying. The way we do this is by asking ourselves a question: "What would I do *if* . . .?" This MAGIC IF, Stanislavski has shown us, is the key to understanding the role you play.

Now let us say you are asked to play the part of a king or queen in a particular play. How would you go about it? If you wished to portray the character truly and well, you would not merely get up and say a lot of lines the playwright has written for the character. You would wish to know more about that king or queen before you began so that you could give him an individuality all his own. You would wish to portray him in such a way that your audience would believe, for the duration of the play, that you are that king or queen. There is a way to do this well, and it is quite simple to learn.

First you must ask yourself Stanislavski's famous question: WHAT WOULD I DO IF I were the king or queen in this particular situation — not merely an actor playing the part; but if I were *really* and *truly* the king or queen? Now you will find you have lots of help from the playwright; he has written the moves of your character as well as the words your character is to speak, and he has given you the circumstances in which you are to act out the part of the king or queen. You also will undoubtedly have other actors onstage to help get the scene across to the audience. All you, the actor, have to do then in order to make your character believable is to continue to utilize the MAGIC IF.

For example, if you are playing the king or queen and you see by your script that the King or Queen crosses the room and kneels before the altar — before you make that move, you would ask yourself, "What would I do if I were this king? Why am I crossing to the altar?" And then if your next line is a prayer for your troops, let us say, you might think, "I suddenly thought of the troops going into battle today — for my country — and since everything depends upon them, I want to pray for them — to ask protection for them from a higher power than myself." This answer you have thus given yourself lends purpose to your movement as you cross the room. You are now not merely wandering blankly across the stage. You now have a purpose for your bodily action. It leads you, logically (with good reason), to the altar where you must now kneel.

When you receive a part, even before you start to learn your lines, go over it with the MAGIC IF in mind. Whatever your character does in the play, ask yourself, "What would I do if . . .?" Just as we did just now with the bodily action of our mythical king or queen, you can structure your part — whatever it may be — if you seek in each case to make your MAGIC IF lead from thought to speech and bodily action. Often the playwright does not inform you why a character does a given thing; he may just say, "The king sits — down left." You see the script merely states the fact of his sitting and where (downstage = the front of the stage and left = the left side) on the stage he is to sit. It is then up to you, the actor, to use your MAGIC

IF to motivate this action — to give it a motive or purpose, a reason for being.

Thus, if you said to yourself, "What would I do if I were the king here? Would I wish to sit down just then? If so, why? Am I sitting because I am tired? Am I sitting to be comfortable while doing something else — such as taking off my boots or chatting with another character? Do I suddenly feel ill? If I were this king, then, why would I sit at this particular moment in the play?" the MAGIC IF will lead you (along with the idea of the play itself) to the proper answer. It will lead you logically to your correct bodily action, and your audience will believe in you as that character if your bodily actions are appropriate. Your audience will have to believe in you if you, yourself, believe in what you are doing. It is that simple. When you use the MAGIC IF, you lead yourself to inner (thought) and outer (bodily-action) truth. And as we discovered in our last lesson, the correct bodily action will help you think and feel like the character you are portraying so that you may go on to the completion of the play with that same assurance (confidence) you gained at the beginning — when you first began to ask the MAGIC IF.

Now I am going to give you some exercises which will help you make good use of that MAGIC IF. Your parent or teacher will watch and take the place of an audience. If you are doing these exercises in your classroom, perhaps your teacher will allow you to perform before the rest of the class so that they can be your audience. You will soon see that if you do not use your MAGIC IF, you may end up acting woodenly, like a stick figure. But if you do utilize the MAGIC IF, you will find your audience stays with you and understands everything you do.

In our exercises you will not have the help of the playwright. You must make up your own words and actions. We do this to sharpen our awareness. If you can do this well without a script, think how much simpler acting will be for you when you actually have a play script and a part already written for you.

Exercise II. *The Magic If . . . .*

1. You are alone in your room; your parents are not at home. For the first time they have trusted you to stay alone and do your homework while they are out for a short walk. You have been doing your homework. **What would you do IF you suddenly smelled smoke?** Let us see what you are doing all the time. Structure the scene as you go along; when you are working on your homework, for instance, think of some actual homework you have done before and go over it in your mind's eye. If you are handling books and pencils and paper, let us *see them*. For us to see them, you must first feel their weight and shape in your hands. Let your hands show us what you are holding. Even though you will not have real "props" (stage properties or actual objects needed in the scene) to work with, you must make your audience see you writing with your imaginary pencil, etc. When you smell the smoke, let us see your reaction first in your facial expression and then in your bodily action. What will you do? Will you just remain there, working and ignoring the possible fire? Will you drop everything and search about the room for the fire? If you find the source of the smoke, what will you do about it? Whatever you do, *think* and then *do*, and we will see through your bodily actions what you are thinking.

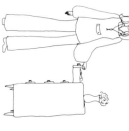

2. You have saved up to buy your mother a birthday present. It is time to go to the store and buy the gift, but when you look in the drawer where you kept the money, you cannot find it. **What would you do IF** the money was missing? Think before you begin. Be sure to let us see everything you do — if you open other drawers, let us feel the weight of those drawers in your hands — they are not made of thin air. Remember: You must actually feel the drawer as you pull it out. If you look about the room in the course of this exercise and peer into closets, let us see the doors you open and close. Whatever you do, remember that we should be able to tell by your bodily actions what the thought behind every action is. We can only see what you put there for us to see.

3. Your teacher has asked you to represent your class at a special Teacher/Student meeting. You go to the room written on your card. **What would you do if** it turned out to be the wrong room? Let us see by your facial expressions and bodily actions what sort of room you have entered . . . what is going on there? How do you know it is not the right room? Keep your bodily actions clear so that your audience can understand what is going on at all times.

Exercise II.

4. This is a very special day for you. All day at school you have been looking forward to the afternoon when you and your family are to leave for a special vacation. Now you enter your house. **What would you do IF your mother told you the trip had been suddenly canceled?** Let us see everything you do. When you enter the house, don't forget to visualize everything. Hang up your outer clothing just as you would in your real home. When you first see your mother, visualize your own mother. And if you incorporate father or sister or brother into your scene, think of the real people whom you actually know.

5. You have been delegated to speak as a representative of your church at a special conference in another town. It is quite an honor, and you are excited about it. You have already boarded the bus. **What would you do IF you suddenly realized you were on the wrong bus?**

6. Now do this again — only this time you make up the story. Where are you going? Why? Whom are you going to meet? Do you know him, or will he be a stranger? **What would you do IF you were: a prince/princess? a spy? a teacher? a beggar with no money for fare?** Use your imagination — but

Exercise II.

> make us, the audience, see from your bodily action just what is taking place.

Practice Project. Here is your *Practice Project* to be prepared at home and performed at the next session where your parent or teacher will be in charge.

All you have to do is this: Pick out one block through which you pass often — every day on your way to school, perhaps. As you go through the street all week, look around you carefully. Use your eyes and your emotions to tell us everything you saw on that one block during the week. Is there ivy growing along one of the walls of a building? Are there overflowing ashcans in front of the buildings? Examine each house, store, sidewalk — how does it look in bright sunlight? Have you ever been there after dark? If so, does it give you a different feeling at night? Is this particular street a pleasant place? Does it make you happy to pass through it? Or is it congested and dreary? How does the street look in rainy, gray weather? How does the street smell? Sound? Tell us all about it at the time of the next lesson.

See if anyone in class can guess what street you are describing. (In working with a parent, try to make him/her see the street. Did your parent guess which one it was?) And don't forget the people on that street. Don't forget to tell us about them. Is there a young housewife with a new baby? How does she behave with her child? Is she very protective? Have you seen an old lady with white hair — a limp — a mole on her cheek? Which foot does she limp with? Could you portray her onstage? How does she make you feel? Even if you do

Practice Project

not know her personally, try to examine her effect on you. Show us before beginning work on the next chapter.

What can YOU do with awareness
and imagination?
. . .A younger, shorter actor. . . .

. . .can portray an older, taller,
more forceful character!

3. Awareness and Imagination

Now we're coming to the real must of our work. The real fun of being an actor goes into these preparations we're about to do now, and what we are going to discuss in this chapter you can use to good advantage whether or not you ever appear on the stage.

Imagination and awareness go hand-in-hand for the actor — and for the ordinary mortal who learns to use his awareness and imagination, life becomes much more interesting and exciting.

If he is going magically to become other people in his roles on the stage or on television, an actor especially must learn to use his awareness to its fullest. He must learn to "read between the lines" of life. You know that a limb which is unused, such as a broken leg, has a tendency to atrophy or become wasted. This is true of your awareness and imagination too. But if you actively look for the sometimes hidden meaning in things, you will be "learning your lines," and reading between them at the same time. If you keep your eyes and ears open, your awareness will grow — so give it a chance to function more often, and you'll find the more you use it, the more efficient it will become. The more you use your imagination, the more it will work for you when you need it — onstage or off.

Here we go right now with a little test for your own awareness and imagination. What do you think would be the first thing for an actor to study to prepare himself? Of course you must have guessed that the study of people is most necessary to an actor. And the person you should know best of all is yourself, naturally. Therefore it is important now to stop and think about yourself — to know as much about you as possible: your likes and dislikes, your ideas and plans, your favorite subjects at school, your hobbies and interests in life. Keeping a diary is helpful here — but it must be a diary of your innermost thoughts and observations, not merely a list of the things you do each day.

Since anyone who wishes to become an actor must make his awareness and imagination a part of his daily experience, watching and listening to other people around you is very important. Take a good look at your mother next time you see her. Don't take her for granted and say, "Oh well, she's mom, that's all." Try to examine her from an outsider's viewpoint. Notice little things about her — the tone of her voice when she's happy, angry, upset; the way she smiles when she is pleased. See if you can discover any habits she may have which you never noticed before. For example, does she twist a strand of hair about her finger when she is deep in thought? You can do this with your teacher at school too. Notice, for instance, whether she bites the end of her pencil when she is concentrating. All these things are the stuff of characterization (creating the character). The more you notice and take down in your mental notebook about the people who are constantly about you in your everyday life, the more you will be storing up a backlog of habits and traits which can be utilized in future roles. Who knows whether a habit you may have noticed first in your little sister may one day become an important part of a role you will be playing on the stage. The more knowledge about other people you store up in your mental storehouse, the better your imagination will be when you call upon it to help you create a new person for a stage characterization.

You will notice that when your teacher gives you a part in a play, the playwright does not tell you about your character's past, as a rule. Some of the character's "present" is all he mentions, leaving his past and his future alike to the actor's imagination. This means you will have to use your awareness and imagination to create a fully rounded character when you are preparing your role. That is what makes it so important for us to sharpen our awareness and make use of our imagination to try to understand people — their reasons for doing what they do and their behavior in various situations. The actor must learn to judge what is good and what is bad in his characterization, so that he can keep in only the good and useful pieces of business (bits of stage action) he has planned for the role and discard (get rid of) extraneous or unnecessary actions. In other words, he must become selective, choosing only what seems right for the character.

Now let us stop for a moment and discuss the creation of a well-rounded character. When you fill in the missing pieces of a playwright's puzzle, you help to create a whole person. When you give your character a past, present and future, you make him real to the audience. So you must first think about your character such thoughts as "Where was he born? What kind of a home did he grow up in? Was he always what he seems to be now (at the time of the play), or did some circumstance in his past life help to change him into what he now is?" Thus, as you work on your part, you are creating — forming — a new human being, giving him a past and thinking about what his hopes might be for the future as well. If you have taken your character beyond the boundaries set by the playwright, you have begun to create a character which will be strictly your own. Only then can your characterization enhance or enrich the work of the playwright. Thus the author and the actor work hand-in-hand to create a really good performance.

A diamond has many sides or facets. So does a human being. Therefore the actor finds many facets to the creation of any character. Besides having some idea of your character's past and future, you must go beyond the playwright's hints in familiarizing yourself with his present. That is, you must know him in the now. How old is he? What sort of person is he? What are the little idiosyncrasies or habits peculiar to him alone? Besides his voice, which we will discuss at length in Chapter Six, what else is important in the building of your character? What about his size and shape? Have you ever watched a fat man walking up the stairs? A thin man? What differences can you see in the way they walk? Could you portray a fat man onstage without any padding or costume to help you? And if you should happen to be plump yourself, can you portray a thin person? If you will watch next time you see a fat person, you will notice that the difference between his carriage (the way he walks) and that of a thin man is in the way he balances himself. Someone who carries a lot of weight, particularly weight concentrated in the stomach area, has to balance that weight over his legs. The legs therefore will usually be wider apart, to support the weight, and often he tends to lean backwards a bit to allow his protruding stomach to precede him as he moves.

We will talk of age differences in a later chapter, but in your preparations to sharpen your awareness and imagination, you must be aware and imaginative about your character's age, voice, speech, etc., right along with all the other things you notice about him. Look at an old man. Is he steady on his feet? Do his shoulders sag as if with the weight of the world? Does he seem somehow to fold in the middle? Do all old people walk the same way, or are some more vigorous than others? Pay attention to any older people you see — visit your grandparents if possible.

And as you observe people, don't forget to *listen* too. Although we'll talk more about voice later, think now, while developing your awareness, about the *cadence* (the lilt or pattern) of a person's speech. Your audience is affected not only by *what* your character says but also *how* he says it. You must therefore pay attention to the *coloring* of the words, the *intonation* or pitch of voice with which he speaks, the *contrast* in tone between different thoughts your character verbalizes and, above and beyond all this, the *silences* or pauses which also have a bearing on the meaning and emotional content of what he says. Stanislavski constantly told his pupils how important it was to create inner pictures for the words they were speaking. (If you asked a fellow actor, "Please bring me an apple," would you not see in your mind's eye the *action*, the *picture* of that person actually bringing the apple to you?) This is what Stanislavski meant when he said, "To an actor a word is not just a sound, it is the evocation [bringing out] of images."

Think about all the elements you will be bringing together, then, when you create your character. Be aware of everything about him, and let your imagination have free rein before you select from your experience of yourself and others what you will need in order to bring the character you are playing to life — his own, special life.

Exercise III. *Awareness and Imagination*

1. Using your observations of people, create a short, heavy set woman (man if you're a boy) having a heated discussion with a tall, old man. Though the second person is not actually there, let us see this man's height by your action. Will you have to keep straining your neck to look up at him? Will your voice grow louder or softer as you argue? Think about everything and show us the scene.

2. You have just stepped out of the swimming pool, and the sun is low in the sky. You are cold and cannot find your bathrobe. You are an older person and suffer from arthritic pains in your neck whenever you are exposed to the cold. You enlist the aid of a friend at the poolside to help you find your robe. Think. If you are dripping wet, shivering and in pain, will this make a difference in your voice? In what kind of temper will you be? How will you go about persuading the other person to help you? Will you be argumentative or friendly? Will your condition have anything to do with your attitude? What will you be doing with your hands? Feet? Body?

Before we get to our *Practice Project*, let's take a minute to sum up what we have learned in this chapter.

Exercise III.

Do you remember the three things the Giant's wife felt really belonged to Jack and so gave him to take back with him in the old fairytale *Jack and the Beanstalk?* The little red hen who laid a golden egg every day, the magic carpet that could take him anywhere and the magic lyre which played beautiful music without human hands.

When you become aware of the things in your world, ideas (golden eggs) are born which help you in your activities. And your imagination is the "magic carpet" of the same tale: It can take you anywhere your mind conceives. When you use awareness and imagination *together,* the combination brings the harmony represented by the magic lyre which could play only beautiful music.

Practice Project. We will be discussing the action of the voice in portraying old age more fully in Chapter Six, but since we are here concerned with imagination and awareness, let us see how well you can do on your own, creating an old man if you are a boy, an old woman if you're a girl. Notice the differences when you come in contact with older people, in the sounds of their voices, the way they walk. A really old person rarely walks with the same sure, fast gait of a younger one and may be somewhat bent over from arthritis or other diseases of old age; he may even need a cane to help him walk. So examine an old person this week and see if you can make him come to life in your session with parent/teacher next time. The scene in this case is not important; what you say is not that important either for this exercise — but you must make up a scene, and words to say in that situation will come to you. Show us the

Practice Project

old man or woman so clearly that we will believe in your performance of age.

Select a speech of any of the characters in a book of plays. Examine the speech at home, going over the lines to show how silences or pauses can change the meaning of the words. Read it over in several different ways to show the contrast and change in the words' meaning that slow speech can make. Accelerate or speed up your speech. Pause at unexpected places. Pause at expected places. Does the meaning change? At your next session bring in the speech and read it in the various ways you have practiced. Your teacher or parent will be able to see the differences you have discovered.

You should become aware of the larger
area around you gradually —
going from the limited area
of the small circle of attention
about you to. . . .

A large circle of attention
is everything you.
the actor. can see onstage.

the medium circle of attention containing objects farther away, to . . .

the large circle of attention that takes in the whole stage.

4. Concentration: Circles of Attention

Years ago, when the actors at the Moscow Art Theatre (the theatre in which Stanislavski worked) first started learning the Stanislavski system they took some time for preparation — a period of "concentration" — before they began acting. Nowadays we know better. Actors who use the Stanislavski system today purposely discuss other subjects just before they begin a performance, since they have proven to themselves that after practicing, they are able to concentrate on any object they wish when they wish.

It's all a matter of learning. When we learn the art of concentration, then we, too, shall be able to concentrate *at will*.

Today we shall find out how to make concentration a simpler matter, and we shall start by learning about Stanislavski's "circles of attention." Stanislavski has shown us how we can best concentrate our attention on our bodily action by limiting attention to different parts of the stage at any given time. He set these "circles of attention" by using objects on the stage as boundaries:

1. *A small circle of attention:* A limited area which includes you, the actor, and a few objects around you, such as a chair or bench, etc. In the *small circle of attention* you, the actor, are the center of this small area and can therefore direct your attention easily to the objects within your small circle.

2. A medium circle of attention: A larger area which may take in several actors and groups of objects (for instance, a table and chair). You, the actor, should become aware of this medium circle gradually — do not try to see it all at once.

3. A large circle of attention: Everything you, the actor, are able to see on the stage. Naturally, the larger the circle of attention, the more difficulty you will have in keeping your attention centered. Therefore, when you are onstage and you feel your attention wandering, direct it to a single thing (a wall clock, a vase, etc.) and concentrate on that. When you have succeeded, you may then direct your attention first to a small circle, then to a medium circle, and then on to a large one.

Now let us think about this for a moment. An actor's concentration obviously is not limited to what he can see onstage. We must also sharpen the concentration on sounds we hear as well as images in our minds. You will recall our discussion of the "evocation of images" in the previous chapter. You must spend some time learning to concentrate on the sounds you hear — and the images they make in your mind. When you have learned to concentrate successfully, you will be active both inwardly and outwardly, and the activity will lead you to the point where you are able to "switch on" the mechanism of your emotions or feelings.

We will talk more about the emotions later. Now, before we get to the *Practice Project* which is designed to help you in your private efforts to concentrate at will, we will perform some exercises with sounds and images which will not only help to make you a better actor when you appear in your next school play but — even more exciting — will also help you develop a more acute and sensitive sense of hearing in your everyday life.

Exercise IV. *Concentration*

1. Sit with your back to your teacher or parent. Have the teacher/parent make a sound behind you, and see if you can identify it.

2. Sit quietly and *listen*. Tell how many different sounds you hear: a dog barking, a sneeze, a heavy truck or bus passing the building, the honking of horns in the traffic outside, the sound of rain on the windowpane if it should be raining, the hissing of a radiator, the hum of a refrigerator if you are doing this exercise at home, or the sounds of the other classrooms if you are in school — doors opening or shutting, a class reciting in another room. You will soon find that even in the quietest room there is no absence of sound.

3. Examine an object close by. Find out everything about it: its size, shape, color, etc. Then turn your back on it, and describe what you remember about the object. Do the same with an object a short distance away. Do the same with an object across the room. This exercise will help you learn how to use your circles of attention to concentrate.

4. Concentrate on an object. Then slowly change the direction of your attention to the small, medium and finally the large circles of attention and then back again to the original object.

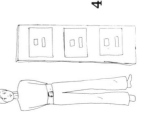

33

Exercise IV.

If you practice, you will find your powers of concentration improving every day; as with all exercises — practice makes perfect! Here, then, is your *Practice Project:*

Practice Project. Pick out any object that belongs to you. Put it on your bed or on the table and sit down and look at it — no matter what is going on in the rest of the house. Even if the TV set is on — ignore it while you do this exercise. If a baby sister or brother is crying or if a neighbor is shouting — ignore everything else around you. Put the object down and examine it carefully. Then make up an imaginary story about the object and be prepared to tell it to your teacher or parent next time. For example, if the object is a comb, think that it once belonged to one of the *Beatles*. Try to see it all in your imagination . . . how and when he used it . . . where he was going when he combed his hair with it, etc. This is only an example. You make up your own story and use your own object.

OUR SENSES tell us more when we train them. Cut off one sense and the others take over to become keener. Without *sight...*

Smell it and find out more...

Touch is the first to discover a familiar food. But is it really what we think?

Taste it. Sweet or sour?

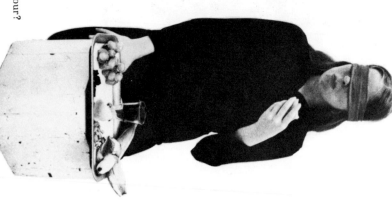

Hear the laughter! Of course—
you knew it was
a lemon all the time.
ALL your senses
contribute to give
you the answer.
when you're not sure.

5. Using Your Five Senses

Just as you use all of your five senses to help you in your everyday life, you may use them to help you in your life as an actor on the stage.

Everything an actor sees, touches, hears, smells and tastes is important in creating the character he must play. All of these senses are like seeds the actor plants. From these seeds grow the flourishing plant (well-rounded character) or the choking weed (one-dimensional character). Later we will discuss the memory of feelings and how an actor uses the feelings brought back to him by remembering the way he felt earlier when he saw, touched, heard, smelled or tasted something in the past. But first let us try to make much fuller use of our senses so that they will grow and expand. Only in that way will we be able to depend upon them when we need their help. As we use them more fully, they will serve us more completely.

You, as the actor, will be using your senses onstage as well as off. The character you create is also a human being, and in taking on his character, you will see, touch, hear, smell and taste all the things he must come in contact with within the play.

If your character is called upon to eat a meal onstage — let us say it is a breakfast of fried eggs — and you can't stand fried eggs, what will you do? (You will probably not actually eat fried eggs in any case, since onstage more durable foods are usually substituted for the "real thing" which is too perishable — and often impossible to cook backstage.) You will remember your MAGIC IF and eat as *if* you loved them. In *Life with Father*, a play with a long run on Broadway some years ago, the family sat down to breakfasts of rich, orangey apricots in place of eggs at every performance. Yet they had to give the impression they were eating fried eggs. Therefore, even though you may be chewing a mouthful of apricot, your audience must feel it is a mouthful of eggs. And whether or not you, personally, like eggs (or even apricots), if the character you play does, you must show by your facial expression and your bodily action that you are enjoying the meal. So what you'll be doing is substituting the memory of a taste you really do enjoy for the one you are actually experiencing. It is really similar to our work with objects made of "air" — when we rehearse combing our hair without a comb, all the while showing the audience the size and shape of the comb by the way we hold our "air" comb. We will discuss this sort of thing more fully in Chapter Eight, when we talk about *Truth on the Stage*. However, for now let's get to using our five senses.

Taking our onstage "breakfast scene," how do we use our other senses — besides "taste" — here? All of them come into play, naturally. You use your sight — seeing the breakfast table, dishes, other actors in the scene and of course, the "eggs." You see before you what appears to be a plate of fried eggs. However, you *know* they are really apricots. Nevertheless they must *look* like eggs to you and to your audience. With your MAGIC IF you will then see them as *if* they were eggs. Then you will see only eggs. As you cut into them with your knife and fork, you are using your sense of *touch*. A knife, you know, will cut through a fried egg quickly, easily, whereas it must take a bit longer and be a bit slower to cut through a pulpy apricot. Your MAGIC IF will let you feel the movements of the knife and fork *as if* they were cutting through eggs. Now how does the sense of *hearing* fit into the stage picture we've conjured up here? The sound of the knife and fork cutting easily through your "eggs" will come to your ears if you have used your MAGIC IF to hear the utensils cutting *as if* they were cutting eggs. Now in this case you will not be able to use your ordinary sense of *smell*, since the object before you does not smell like eggs. In fact, does an apricot smell much at all? Nevertheless, for the sake of producing the truth of your stage action for your audience and helping them to feel that the character you are playing is really eating and enjoying a delicious-smelling breakfast, your sense of smell must come into play as well.

Here, then, are some exercises to help develop your various senses so that they will be alert and dependable and ready to cooperate with your MAGIC IF.

Exercise V. The Senses

1. **Sight:** Your parent or teacher will prepare a tray containing ten objects covered with a cloth or towel. Without removing the covering, place the tray on your lap as you sit comfortably in a chair. Close your eyes for a moment before beginning and relax. Now open your eyes and remove the covering, examining every object on the tray. Do not pick anything up — merely look at each thing and try to observe everything about it, including its shape, color, size, etc. Cover the tray again and try to tell your teacher or parent what you saw. How many objects can you describe? How much can you remember about each one? Now do it again. This time how many did you remember?

2. **Touch:** Your parent/teacher will ask you to close your eyes or put on a blindfold. He/she will then put various objects (one by one) into your hands [not the same objects as in the previous exercise]. Examine them only with your sense of touch. Feel everything. Turn each object over in your hands until you can describe its texture (is it hard, soft, warm, cold?), its shape, size and whatever else you can tell about it. If you do not do so well the first time you try this, you may repeat similar exercises at home during your *Practice Project* time, having a friend or relative hand you various objects until you have developed your sense of touch more fully.

Exercise V.

3. **Sound:** Your parent/teacher will have you close your eyes or put on a blindfold. She/he will make a series of sounds in the room. You are to describe them and tell us what you think they are.

4. **Taste:** The teacher/parent will bring to class a group of foods which you must taste with eyes closed or blindfolded. As you taste each one, think about the flavor. Is it sharp? Sweet? Bitter? Tangy? Now, after describing it, try to tell what food you have tasted.

5. **Smell:** Still blindfolded or with closed eyes, you will be given a series of objects to sniff. You must not touch them — merely smell them. Now tell us what they smell like and identify each one.

"My eyes hurt!"
Can you hear the voice
of the child in the sandbox?

6. Extending Your Senses: Voice

Now that we have worked on using our senses to the greatest possible extent, we are going to try actively to extend those senses by making use of them in conjunction (in combination) with other things. In this chapter we are going to discuss VOICE. What is a voice? It seems to fit into the category of SOUND. It is the sound we make when we speak. Other people's voices reach our ears, and we make use of our sense of *hearing* to understand them. Our own voice, in turn, is one of our most important communicators: With it we try to make use of the sense of hearing in our listeners to get across our message. Therefore it is the combination of speaking and hearing in conjunction with *language* that gets our spoken message across. There are many ways an actor uses his voice in his characterizations. In our *Practice Project* for today you will be using your voice to help create an old woman or an old man. But before we come to that part of our work, let us take time out now to talk a little about changing the voice and how it is done.

First of all, do not try to do it without a model to guide you. That is, you must be thinking about a *specific* person if you wish to recreate him or her. Never do things in general — always be *specific*. Find a person who fits your character's needs or create him by using traits from several different people you know to build one whole character of your own.

Like fingerprints, the voice is a very personal part of you. Nobody else in the world has exactly the same voice as you do. This makes it especially helpful to actors to be able to listen to and simulate the voice of (pretend to talk like) someone else. You can personalize your part so much better if you use your voice to help form the new person you create for your stage character.

Did you know that our larynx (vocal cords) was not meant to help us to speak? Birds have a vocal organ called the "syrinx" which is exclusively used to produce sound. Man does not have this organ but has learned to adapt his vocal cords for that purpose instead of using them exclusively in their true biological function: to help us to breathe normally, to hold our breath and to guard the passageway to the lungs from foreign matter. Man has added another function — he has adapted his larynx to the task of creating the voice.

It was man who discovered that if his taut (tight) vocal muscles vibrated as exhaled air flowed over them, sound was produced. Thus it was that man, who is "higher than the animals," adapted this biological organ to social use — he used it to "communicate" with other men. For as he began to create words by refining his first cries into meaningful sound symbols (or words), he created a means of communication that still helps him to reach others and allows him to release pent up emotions, such as he does in crying, sobbing, laughing or sighing. Now he is even able to make music (singing, humming). He can laugh, hum, sing or scream as well as speak — something none of the lower animals have been able to do.

It is through such acts as screaming, sighing, singing and crying that we reveal our emotions to others. You can see that that is why the voice is such an important instrument for the actor — who must get meanings across in ways other than mere speech. An actor must therefore learn to control the use of his voice. Learn to control your voice and you learn to control your audience — to move them in the way you wish them to feel.

So what have we discovered? Besides the actions of your body on the stage, you have the instrument of your voice to help you create a character. Now listen to this: *Voice reveals age!* We already know that fact from our everyday lives, but we must know it in a special way for our stage life. The voice can tell many secrets about its owner — the most important being his age. From the lusty cry of a newborn infant to the weak sigh of a tired old lady, the voice ages along with the rest of our bodies.

(1) When a newborn child cries, the doctor is happy because he knows the passageway to his lungs is open and he is breathing and healthy. If a baby does not cry at birth, the doctor often slaps him to make him cry, just for the purpose of hearing the sound that tells him the airway to the child's lungs is working.

(2) Throughout babyhood and childhood the voice in boys as well as girls is high-pitched and usually loud.

(3) In adolescence or the beginning of the teenage cycle, the voices of both girls and boys change to a lower pitch. But this is more noticeable in boys, and sometimes a boy's voice, during this period, is still unstable — causing a sudden squeak to come forth in the midst of lower-pitched sounds. This is when people say, "His voice is changing." This is because the vocal cords (larynx) undergo an actual physical change during this period. They become longer and thicker so that a lower pitch is necessarily produced when vibrations touch them.

(4) In adults the voice has been stabilized at this lower pitch. Usually it remains that way throughout adulthood until the onset of old age changes the pitch once again — to higher, squeakier tones. Thus, if you were playing an adult, you would have to try to lower your voice to attain the proper sound, whereas if you were playing a doddering old man, you would raise the pitch of your voice to indicate extreme age.

You can readily see that from the time you were born till the time you grow old and die, your voice carries your own special individuality just as your fingerprints do. This means that your voice mirrors your moods — whether you are sick or well, whether you are young or old or in between and of course whether you are male or female. And because your voice belongs to you alone, you can be identified by your voice. Haven't you ever answered the telephone to hear a "hello" from the other end whose owner you could recognize, even though the caller did not give his name? Let's say it was your father calling from work. Didn't you know him immediately? That's because his voice is peculiarly his own just as yours is your own. So you can see that the broader the range you can give to your voice for the stage, the more chance you have of creating completely "different" people for each of your roles. Give this some thought the next time you receive a part to perform in a school play. See if by any chance a slight change in your voice might not alter the characterization you create in such a way as to make it more *believable*.

Now we come to our exercise for today. Since we have been talking today about the *action of voice* as differentiated from *bodily action*, this time let's work on the voice itself.

You know that the author's words are dead until the actor breathes life into them in the role of the character. The actor therefore must analyze his lines to bring out the meaning the author intended — *but he must bring it out in the voice of the character he portrays* — the person the author has put down on paper.

Exercise VI. The Action of the Voice:

Even a simple sentence, such as "My eyes hurt," can have as many different meanings as there are characters who might say it or moods of one character who says it. Use your *awareness* and *imagination* (turn back to Chapter Three if you want to brush up on the use of awareness and imagination before beginning) to say this phrase, "My eyes hurt," in different ways, giving it different meanings for each character. Remember the age level.

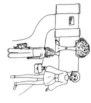

1. An old lady confined to a wheelchair and living in an institution fretfully says, "My eyes hurt," to the attendant who has placed her chair in front of a sunlit window.

2. A young boy is doing his homework in a poorly lit room. He stops and rubs his eyes. His mother calls to him to ask why he is not finishing his work. His answer: "My eyes hurt!"

3. A little child is playing in a sandbox. He gets sand in his eyes. He begins to cry, "My eyes hurt." (Don't forget to utilize your voice in the proper way to indicate the age of the character. Let's hear the voice of a toddler here.)

4. A mother is outdoors walking with her child on a windy day. Suddenly a bit of dirt is blown into the woman's eyes, and she immediately lets go of the

Exercise VI.

_____

child's hand to protect her injured eyes. The child inquires what the trouble is, and she replies, "My eyes hurt." (How old is the mother? Remember an adult's voice is stabilized at a lower pitch than yours. Try to achieve the proper voice.)

The following will give you an opportunity to try to create the voices of old age:

1. An old witch cackles as she pets her cat, "What ho, my pretty? What's wrong with you today? You're acting as though some spirits had gotten into you, little one. Come, come, let me see a happy face. Let's hear you purr now, and I'll give you a nice, juicy gizzard for your supper!"

2. A very old lady sits rocking her great grandchild. She sings the old lullaby: "Rockabye baby in the treetop — when the wind blows the cradle will rock. When the bough breaks the cradle will fall — down will come baby, cradle and all." (Show the woman's age within the confines of the song. Is it easier than in spoken words? Harder?)

3. An old professor has received a going away gift from his students, as he is retiring today. He makes the following acceptance speech: "Thank you —

Exercise VI.

thank you all. It is difficult for me to control my emotions today — you have all been so wonderful. Your gift is delightful, and I will treasure it. And now, before I leave, may I give you a little gift in return. It is simply a small piece of advice from my own experience. 'The good men do lives after them. The evil is as quickly forgotten as the man who causes it.' If you will always think of the pleasant things you can do for others, as you have to-day with this lovely gift you have given your old professor, there will be no room for unhappiness in your life.''

Practice Project. Today I want you to use your awareness and imagination to think about extending your own senses. We've been talking about the use of voice as such an extension. Before your next session with your teacher/parent, extend your imagination and awareness to help you discover other ways you can extend your senses. Do you think *painting* extends them? Playing a musical instrument? Reading books? Talking to friends? Suppose you play a little game with one of your friends between now and your next class. Have the friend ''speak'' to you without ''words.'' In other words, have him or her merely mouth the words without sound (as in pantomime). You watch carefully and see if you can read the friend's lips. Now try it the other way 'round; you speak without sound and let your friend try to read your lips. Tell us about it next time.

Think too, particularly, about your sense of smell. You wouldn't think the sense of smell

Practice Project

could have much to do with acting, but it does. This week try to develop that sense. When your mother has a pizza in the oven, for instance, what does this aroma do to you? It fills you with a sense of anticipation — a looking forward to the taste of the food you know is cooking at the moment. It can even make your mouth "water." So when you like the object that you *smell* cooking in the oven, it gives you a sense of well-being to anticipate the taste of the food. Then, it also builds your *memory of feelings*. In Chapter Seven we shall talk more about the *memory of feelings*, but let me just remind you now that the pizza you smell cooking — which gives you such a good feeling even before you eat it — will come back to your "feeling memory," at a later time — when you may again smell another pizza being cooked. The delicious odor triggers off the previous memory and helps you to recall the first time you ate the pizza. This can also, of course, work in reverse with an unpleasant odor — or even a pleasant one which you smelled at a time when you were already sad or angry or upset. This sort of thing, too, is a way of extending your senses. Let's see what original ways you have used to extend yours when you next see your teacher/parent. Tell us about it then.

Clap your hands at the theatre.
Are you merely being polite?
Or did you truly enjoy
the performance?

7. The Memory of Feelings

We spoke earlier of using our senses to the fullest. In Chapter Six we found that even the sense of smell can help the actor to create his role by reminding him of what he felt at another time when he smelled the same odor. We were talking about the memory created by the sense of smell. Today we shall explore this type of memory further. This is what is called "emotional memory," or the memory of feelings. Things you see, hear, smell, touch or taste can remind you of feelings you had in the past.

Emotional (feeling) memory brings back past experiences which can be helpful to an actor in creating a character. When you relive these past experiences onstage though, you must remember to use logical bodily actions. Let us say you recall how you felt at the time a dearly loved pet died. If you are playing the part of a character who has just had the same or a similar experience, you can use this emotional memory for your role . . . but it must be done through bodily action so your audience too will feel your emotion. You might kneel down to gently stroke the animal's fur one last time before the body is removed. Then let us say the script calls for you to sit down and cry. How would you walk to the chair? In a carefree, sprightly manner, or dejectedly, shoulders slumped, your body moving slowly, sadly? The correct bodily action triggers the correct emotional reaction . . . and when you create a scene using correct bodily action as well as correct emotional reaction, your audience becomes part of that scene — lives it with you.

You will recall our discussion of bodily actions in Chapter One. If you have been keeping up with our work, you should have had much experience in executing logical bodily actions by now. You may turn back to Chapter One and review it briefly, if you wish.

The thing to remember is once you have recalled a particular feeling, you cannot act it out without thinking first of your logical bodily action in the given character of the play. Always the rest of the elements of the Stanislavky system, about which we have been talking in our work, are grouped around the bodily action to help make it logical and truthful and put it in its proper order. All the other elements of Stanislavski's system — such as the "Magic If," awareness and imagination, etc. — will also help the bodily action "turn on" or stir your feelings. Feelings are easily forgotten, but bodily actions can stir them to memory once again.

In Chapter Three we spoke at length about awareness and imagination. You began to notice little things about the people around you to which you had never paid attention before. We said these habits which you stored away in your memory could be useful to you later on-stage . . . that some of them could become part of your character's own personality. If an actor understands people's behavior — the way their minds work, their actions and gestures — he can use these in characterizations in similar situations. All you have to do is to be alert: Watch, listen and remember your own inner feelings as well as what goes on in the world around you. This is how to make your emotional memory work for you.

We have the help of all our senses when we use our emotional memory in all its areas — sight, hearing, smell, taste and touch. *Visual* memory can make us see a person we have forgotten. Have you ever seen a person on the street, for instance, whose way of walking reminded you of someone you knew? Or someone whose appearance resembled one of your friends? That stranger stirred your *visual memory* of another person.

We can *hear* things that remind us of other, long-forgotten things or people — music we have heard before, voices which remind us of people we once knew. The sound of a dentist's drill may remind us of a particularly painful filling we once had. The sound of a slap can make us think of a long-forgotten spanking. The sound of a car's motor may bring back an automobile trip that was fun.

When you have your first date, you will find that holding hands (the sense of *touch*) will have a special meaning that you will hold in your sense memory well into the future. The *taste* and *aroma* (smell) of a new dish at dinner will come back to you next time you eat that same food. Our senses of sight, hearing, smell, taste and touch, then, can make us relive vividly sensations experienced in the past.

Though these remembered sensations may be pleasant or unpleasant, we must learn to use them for our stage roles. But did you know you could use them to help you in real life as well as on the stage? Suppose you were badly frightened — in order to help you get over your fright, you might think of another time when you were frightened but brave . . . when you did something you didn't think you'd be able to do. If you could remember how you acted when you were brave, you could use that memory to help you act bravely again — and soon you'd be *feeling* that way too.

However, since this book is primarily concerned with acting, we will concentrate now on how the memory of feelings helps us to be better actors.

We have talked about two places from which you, as an actor, may draw your material for creative work: your own inner life and the world around you. The inner and outer worlds of an actor should not exist separately but should be used together. In other words, you can't draw material for your role only from within yourself — your own experiences — you must also find inspiration from the things and people around you in the outside world. Writers do this to people their books with fully rounded characters. Stanislavski himself, when he appeared on the stage, used the experiences of his friends and acquaintances to help him create the characters he played. He felt his own feelings and thoughts should be tied closely to his impressions of other people and the outside world. And his success in the parts he played proved that he was right.

When he was ill and knew himself to be dying, he still worked with his students and felt it his duty to pass on to them all he knew about acting. During the last rehearsals he ever attended, he told his actors to pay attention to what he had taught them. He told them to learn to perform the simplest bodily actions, as the logic (sound sense) and proper order of these bodily actions would create within the actors the inner experiences they needed to play their parts well. He explained that carrying out the logic or sense behind a bodily action would automatically help students to understand and create the logic of their feelings. This, he said, was everything for an actor.

Now that we have talked about the memory of feelings and how Stanislavski's students learned to use that memory through bodily action, I am going to give you an exercise which will help you to use your own *memory of feelings* through bodily action.

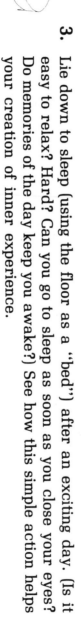
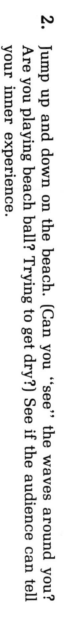
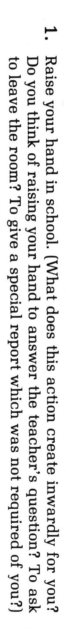

Exercise VII. *From Bodily Actions to Inner Experience*

1. Raise your hand in school. (What does this action create inwardly for you? Do you think of raising your hand to answer the teacher's question? To ask to leave the room? To give a special report which was not required of you?)

2. Jump up and down on the beach. (Can you "see" the waves around you? Are you playing beach ball? Trying to get dry?) See if the audience can tell your inner experience.

3. Lie down to sleep (using the floor as a "bed") after an exciting day. (Is it easy to relax? Hard? Can you go to sleep as soon as you close your eyes? Do memories of the day keep you awake?) See how this simple action helps your creation of inner experience.

4. Clap your hands at the theatre. (Are you merely being polite, or did you truly enjoy the performance?)

5. Your parent/teacher will show you several pictures. Make up a story about each one. For the portraits of people, tell what sort of person each is — what kind of work you think he or she does — how old he is — whether he is single or married — how many children he has, etc. Create a life story

about the person in the picture just as though he were a character in a play. For scenes of country or ocean, tell what mood the picture creates for you — how the scene makes you feel — how you would react if you could suddenly "step into the picture."

And now here is your Practice Project to sharpen your memory of feelings:

Practice Project. Sight. Get out a gift that you received last Christmas. Look at it and try to remember when you first opened it. Examine it as though it were that Christmas morning and you have just seen it for the first time. If you can recreate the actions of that morning, you will soon feel the inner feelings of that day recreated too. When you next come to class, recreate the Christmas scene *without* the actual object. Remember, the correct bodily actions will trigger the correct inner feeling. Make us see the object by the way you handle it, and we will also see your inner feelings in your action.

Hearing. In class or to your parent, tell about a sound that made you remember something out of the past. It might be the hissing of a pressure cooker as mother prepared dinner, reminding you of a previous delicious meal, or one you didn't like. It could be the ring of the doorbell recalling the visit of an old friend some time ago. Church bells might bring back the day a little brother or sister was christened. Keep your ears open and listen. What will you remember?

Practice Project

Smell. Tell the class (or your parent) about a smell you noticed at school or at home which brought back the memory of another encounter with the same odor.

Touch. Bring something to class (or to parent) such as a hairbrush, the small piece of your baby blanket you still keep, an old doll's dress or a model automobile. Explain how the touch of this object recreated in your mind a happy or unhappy experience.

Taste. Tell in class (or to parent) how the taste of something you ate reminded you of another time when you ate the same food in the past. Is it something pleasant or unpleasant? What did it remind you of in your own life?

Now try the same action
with the "real" object
to see how close
you came.

If you learn first
to create physical
actions with "air"
you develop imagination
and concentration.
*Truth on the stage
comes from
belief in what
you are doing.*

Practice without using
actual objects.
Thread a needle

. . .and sew a seam.

8. Truth on the Stage

An *anthropologist* is one who investigates the beginnings and developments, races, customs and beliefs of mankind. Margaret Mead, a great anthropologist of our time, tells the story of a people she studied in New Guinea who have a "system of jerking their heads to induce feeling." The women in this society participate in a ceremony called "second mourning," which is a time, usually a year after the death of a family member, when the family is expected to "mourn" or show sorrow over the death once more. Because so much time has elapsed since the death of the loved one, tears do not come easily. Therefore, the women have perfected this system of jerking their heads to recreate the feeling of sadness they remember having lived through earlier. This seems to help them relive their previous emotions "just as convincingly as they could the day the person died," according to Miss Mead.

We spoke in an earlier chapter about the memory of feelings. Today we are going to discover how you, the actor, can recreate emotions on the stage with truth. Stanislavski worked on this system for many years, revising (changing and perfecting) it so that today you can perform, with the aid of his system, so well that you will be as convincing in your recreated emotions on the stage as those New Guineans were in their period of second mourning, crying real tears a year after a loved one died.

You undoubtedly remember having heard since you were a tiny child the story of George Washington and the cherry tree — how he, as a child, admitted to his father that he'd chopped down the tree because he "could not tell a lie." Onstage we must do a "George Washington" all the time. That is, we must strive to portray the truth of the scene to our audience so that they can *believe* in what we are doing. While an audience is in a theatre, they automatically suspend their sense of the "reality" of things and are willing, for the length of the play, to "believe" in the "truth" of the performance. Of course you know what "truth" is in your everyday life, but did you know that truth on the stage is *different* from truth in real life?

A play is a made-up story — not what really happened — yet it must *appear* true to the audience at the moment they are watching, and this truth must continue throughout the play. Thus you, as the actor, must learn how to make this invention of the playwright into moments of *truth* for your audience. One of the things you will do to accomplish this is to *treat* things or persons onstage *as if* they were what you wish the audience to believe they are.

When you are playing a part onstage, you know your fellow actor is not *really* your father or a king — but you *treat* him as your father or the king if that is what the play is about. You can also treat an object *as if* it were a slithering snake. You can treat a glass of pure water as though it were poison. Once you have developed the ability to treat one person or object *as if* it were another, you have mastered one of the most important lessons of an actor, and you are well on your way to creating truth on the stage. Without this ability you are cheating your audience of the very thing they come to the theatre for — *participation*. To participate, as you know, means to have a share or to take part in something. The audience must take part in what is going on onstage or else the play means nothing. Without their *belief* in what they see onstage, the play will never become real to them. This is the actor's task, then — to create people and incidents or happenings that seem so real at the time that the audience can enter into the spirit of the play and truly believe in what they see while it is happening. This is the way to truth in the theatre. And when I say "the theatre," I do not mean the professional theatre alone. It works the same way in your school auditorium when you are putting on a play for your schoolmates and teachers. It works the same way in any theatre, even if you are performing for your parents or relatives in your own living room. That is a theatre, too, when you use it as such. So, if the "scenic truth" (which is what we call truth on the stage) is essential in the professional theatre, it is equally important in your theatre at school or at home, if the result is to be a good performance — rewarding to your audience and to you, the actor.

Remember to treat your fellow actor *as if* he were whatever person the script calls for — and treat yourself *as if* you were the character in the play. When you do this well and feel *as if* you were doing it in real life, you will be able to enter the state which Stanislavski called "*I am*"; where you merge or become one with the character you are playing. But in trying to create truthful action onstage, you must remember that there are different levels of truth. There can be an uninteresting truth as well as an unusual or interesting truth. In using your action — bodily action, voice and inner action (thought) — onstage, you must always look for the unexpected. Any fuzziness of actions will suspend the audience's belief. They will fail to participate or believe in your character if you do not find unusual forms of truths. For instance, if you were playing the scene of an argument between two characters in your play, you might find that to answer a heated remark with a controlled, quiet reply might be a striking way to present the truth in your action. The contrast or difference between the other character's shouts and your controlled answer could be one of those "unusual" or different actions which can be so impressive onstage. To discover such unusual or different forms of truths, you, the actor, must watch and absorb all impressions around you in your daily life so that you will build up a supply of "possibilities of action" for your future roles. In other words, if you are to draw on your experience to help you play the parts that are assigned to you, you must have as much experience as possible to make a rich, live source for your choice of actions for the stage. You will only be able to treat things as if they were other things if you have experienced those other things. For instance, could you treat a chair as if it were a vicious animal if you had never seen or heard a vicious animal? So keep your eyes and ears open at all times and absorb as much experience in your everyday life as you possibly can. Read as much as you can to get the benefit of the author's creativity, which will stimulate (or start up) your own imagination. Explore your own house and surroundings, but go to as many different places as you can to enrich yourself. Do not be a stranger to libraries, theatres, museums, churches, concerts, art exhibits, etc. Many of these are free. Have your parents or teachers look into the free ones if you cannot afford entrance fees. Or you can do this yourself by checking newspapers and periodicals on what's going on in your town. Ask your parents to take you to these places whenever they can and be particularly alert at school and at home so that impressions of the life all around you will not escape unnoticed. Think about people and let your sense of wonder have full play.

Now here are today's exercises to help you develop truth in your actions onstage:

Exercise VIII. *Truth on the Stage*

1. Treat a chair as another person, a seat on a ride in an amusement park, a barking dog.

2. Treat a pointer (in school) or a broom (at home) as a dancing partner, a dead pet, a sword. Make up a story using these objects, and let us see each object through the story you perform.

3. Drink a liquid as:
   (a) hot chocolate,
   (b) cold milk,
   (c) poison.
   Don't forget to structure a story around each drink. Why are you drinking it? Who are you? What are the consequences or results of drinking each liquid? Do not tell us — show us.

4. Your teacher/parent is going to hide an object in the room while you either close your eyes, are blindfolded or leave the room. Once it is hidden, you may open your eyes or return to the room and search for it. Once you have found it, return it to your teacher or parent who will put it back in exactly the same hiding place with your full knowledge this time. Now re-enter the

room and repeat your search, knowing fully where it is. Remember your MAGIC IF. The second search should have as much suspense as the first.

5. Without using actual objects:
   (a) Open a letter, read it and return it to the envelope.
   (b) Thread a needle and sew a seam.
   (c) Place a book on a shelf.
   (d) Pour a cup of tea.
   (e) **Lift** a boxful of your personal treasures and empty it onto the floor. Now lift the empty box. Structure everything. Would you dump out your treasures roughly or take great care with them?

6. Get dressed for school. Take your time and let us see every article of clothing you put on.

And now, here is your *Practice Project*. Work on this at home.

Practice Project. If you learn to create physical actions without the help of an object (with only "air"), you will develop your concentration, imagination and feeling of truth and belief in what you are doing. Therefore, for your home practice I am going to give you some exercises to help you achieve the highest degree of truthfulness in your actions.

Stanislavski felt exercises like these were as important for the actor as practicing scales on the piano is for a pianist or singing the whole range of notes is for a singer. And the best part is that even if you never set foot on a stage, these exercises will do a lot to make your life more interesting by helping you to develop your imagination and concentration — things that will help you get more out of your everyday life. At your next session with teacher or parent, you must perform these exercises without hesitation without the actual object. You'll find it easy if you rehearse by yourself at home.

For Girls:

1. Open a pocketbook. Reach in and take out a comb. A handkerchief. Use each in turn. Watch and feel everything as you do it. Now put away the pocketbook and do it again — this time without the actual objects. How does the comb feel in your hair? How thick is a handkerchief between your fingers?

For Boys:

2. Bounce a ball up and down — then throw it against a wall and catch it. Watch everything you do. Notice the "feel" of the ball in your hands, the impact when it returns to you. Now do it without using the real ball. How long does it take for the ball to come back? Do your hands move when you catch it?

Both Boys and Girls:

3. Fill a glass with water. Drink. Now put the glass down and do it again with an

Practice Project

imaginary glass and imaginary water. Make sure you "swallow" the imaginary drink. Feel the weight of the full glass in your hand, the partially empty glass.

4. Eat an apple. Be sure to take note of the size of the apple in your hand, its color, shape, etc. As you eat and it grows smaller, do you hold it the same way? **Observe everything.** Then repeat without the actual apple. Can you "taste" the imaginary apple? Is it tart or sweet? How does this register on your face? Feel the texture of the apple between your teeth. Chew the imaginary apple as though it were solid and real.

MUTUAL INFLUENCE. . .what is it?
You are playing with a friend.
Suddenly he takes something
of yours away from you.
What does he do?
Act.
What do you do?. . .

React.

9. Communication and Communion

Today we are going to take up a subject that is just as important to you in your daily life as it is on the stage — communication. What does *communication* mean? The dictionary definition is "giving information or news by speaking or writing." The other word at the heading of this chapter is *communion*, which means "sharing," "having in common," the "exchange of thoughts and feelings."

To show the meaning of his actions to his audience, an actor must *communicate* with his audience through his *communion* with his fellow actors. In other words, he gets the meaning across to the audience by talking to the other actors onstage. He must "give information" to his audience by means of "sharing" with or "exchanging thoughts and feelings" with the other actors in the play.

It has been proven that when an actor acts and reacts to his fellow actors onstage (just as in real life we act and react to the people around us) he holds the attention of the audience completely, and makes them a part of what is going on.

Just as what we do in real life depends upon the people around us, so the character in a play acts and reacts to the other characters who surround him. When you are portraying a character in a school play, you behave in a certain way toward a fellow actor playing a friendly role; but your reaction to a hostile or unfriendly character is quite different. Use your MAGIC IF and your imagination, and you will be able to decide the proper attitude toward all of the other actors who appear in scenes with you. The relationship you develop between yourself and other characters will be an important part of your characterization — the realization and bringing into being of your own role.

Onstage we must never say lines to the other fellow — we must actually communicate with him, as we would in real life. This means (1) to be aware of his bodily presence; (2) to make sure you speak to or touch him and that he understands the speech and/or action; and (3) to make equally sure that you know and understand what he is trying to communicate to you. *Mutual influence* (each working upon the other) is the technical term for this communion between actors. Just as in real life we see images and transmit them through speech to our fellow humans, as they do to us, so it is on the stage.

When you impress on your fellow actor what you want him to see and hear, you cannot help but produce a reaction in the other actor — even if your partner is a bad actor, he must respond. This interplay of communion between actors in turn evokes or creates a response in the audience. However, this works both ways. You, as an actor, must also listen carefully to what your fellow actor says to you. You must hear it as though for the first time — even though you may have rehearsed the scene frequently. During a dialogue (or speech between two characters) you must allow thoughts, plans, memories and decisions to flow freely through your mind, just as you would in real life when someone speaks to you.

While you are speaking to your fellow actor, if you try to create a definite action on his part — such as a laugh, a smile, or even tears — you are aiming for a definite result, and your imagination will take over to help you communicate strongly. If you say something funny to your fellow actor and get him to laugh, for instance, the audience too should see the joke and laugh as well. Think for a moment of your personal life. Aren't there times when you try hard to get something (a treat, a raise in your allowance, a special "role" in a game you're playing with your friends) from one of your parents or playmates? You do not just ask in a haphazard manner if you really want something, do you? No — you put feeling into your request. So it is onstage. You must put feeling behind everything you say to your fellow actor if you wish to communicate fully with him — and you must allow feeling to move you in return when he speaks to you. Otherwise the exchange of dialogue will become very wooden and dull to your audience.

But onstage it isn't always dialogue — sometimes an actor has a part where he talks to himself . . . trying to see or understand his problem better. This is called "soliloquy" (so-lil-o-kwee) and is often used in the theatre to further the action (or forward movement) of a play. Shakespeare used it quite frequently and successfully. You can learn to soliloquize, or talk to yourself onstage, without seeming strange or odd if you will just remember that a monologue or soliloquy reveals the actor's thoughts and feelings to the audience but not to the other characters in the play. Therefore, in preparing your monologue, do as Stanislavski did himself when he was acting. In a way he split himself into two parts — he made the brain and the solar plexus (which is a collection of nerves behind the stomach) talk to each other. Because the brain and the solar plexus are two centers of our nerves' life, he chose to use them as if they were two "myselves" having a dialogue together, like two actors. So if you think of your brain and your solar plexus, if you allow these two important parts of yourself to talk together, your soliloquy will take on added meaning. Remember too that when you have a soliloquy in a play, it is for the benefit of the audience and not your fellow actors . . . it is another way of communicating your inner thoughts and feelings to the audience. If you will enter into it in this spirit, your audience will understand and react properly. So don't be afraid they might laugh at you — they won't — they will enter into the spirit of the soliloquy along with you — and with the same level of intensity or feeling as you put into it.

There are also times onstage when an actor is called upon to communicate with an imaginary object or person. In one of Shakespeare's plays the character Hamlet speaks to a ghost — the ghost of his father. In that play another actor takes the part of the ghost (sometimes speaking from offstage), but if you had to speak to a ghost who wasn't really there — who didn't *appear* at all — could you be convincing? You could if you remembered to use your MAGIC IF — and treated the empty space *as if* there were a creature there to whom you were speaking.

Another way you communicate onstage is by your handling of props (stage properties is their full name). These are objects used in a play that become part of the action. If you played a criminal, for instance, your gun would be a "prop," and how you handled it would be an indication to your audience of how advanced or proficient a criminal you were. Therefore, you would have to practice gun handling until the gun no longer was a foreign object to you, if you intended to communicate to the audience that you really were an experienced criminal. A cup and saucer can be props. So can a letter or a book — or whatever you use in the course of a play, including objects like pieces of furniture. Anything you can handle and that you use personally on stage (a handkerchief, magazine, baseball, etc.) is usually called a "hand prop," and anything your character is to use personally is called a "personal prop." Other, larger objects, such as a radio that must be turned on by your character during the show or a clock which you must pick up and wind at one point in the action, are called "set props," and in Broadway shows they're placed in position by stagehands and checked before every performance. There is usually a "prop table" backstage where the stage manager assembles all the "personal props" before the performance, and it is the actor's responsibility to be sure all the personal props he will be using are ready. Some Broadway actors keep important personal props in their dressing rooms. If you will practice handling all your props before the play is performed, you will be much more at home with them during the actual performance; so spend some time learning how to handle your props when you rehearse for school plays.

Another thing you should do when you have a part to study is to try to find someone to work with you on your lines — your mother, a brother or sister or a friend. This is important in studying dialogue, since you must learn to respond to the other characters in the play. If you study alone all the time, you will become used to getting no answer, no reaction to your lines, and this may make it difficult for you when you actually appear onstage. It is important, therefore, to practice dialogue with another person so you can get the feel of your partner's responses or reactions to your lines. Remember that acting, for the most part, is a *cooperative venture*, where you generally are not alone on the stage but in contact with your fellow actors. And if you work together properly, you will soon find you and your fellow actors create the proper responses in one another just as any two or three people in real life act and react to one another. A slight change in the tone of voice of one will bring about change in the other.

Even in crowd scenes with many people onstage at once, an actor may communicate with various people in the crowd, or all of them. In Stanislavski's theatre even the actors who had no lines to say at all were instructed to create life stories of the characters they portrayed — thus actors who merely appeared onstage in mass scenes or mob scenes, without a single word to say, communicated real feelings because they had created characters who were fully rounded — characters with past, present and future lives — and just as real for the length of the performance as real human beings. Think about a TV program for a minute. Often there are people in street scenes who have no lines at all — they are just passersby — but if these actors have created backgrounds of age, occupation, interests, etc., for themselves, even those minor "walk-on" roles seem to have a life of their own. So you see, any part is what you make it, whether you are the "star" of the show or have just a "bit" part to perform. And be sure that if you start small — with "bit" parts — and really give them characterization, you will soon be asked to perform more important roles.

So don't forget your MAGIC IF, and your awareness and imagination. Remember what we discussed in Chapter Three — how you can create past, present and future plans for your character to make him real. Turn back to Chapter Three now and review it. It will help keep the method of constructing a character for the stage fresh in your mind.

Exercise IX. Actions and Reactions

1. You are playing with a friend. Suddenly he takes something of yours away from you. What do you do? Play this out as it would happen in real life . . . try to remember what happened in a similar situation in your own life. How did you react? Do it now. (The second child will also react to your reaction, and this will create an interesting scene.)

2. You are a spy. You've been instructed to contact another secret agent at a large party where a detective will be present. You must receive from the other agent a certain object — but you have no idea what the other agent looks like. The only means of identification you will have is a prearranged code. You are to use the words, "I wonder what's in the bouquet?" and when you find the right partner he will know the code and reply, "Roses, I think." Only to the person who answers correctly will you make your identity known, and then he will give you the package. You must remember throughout this exercise that there is a detective present whose identity you do not know either. At the end of this exercise your teacher and the rest of the class, who will portray guests at the party, will let you know if anyone discovered what you were doing. If the detective discovers your act during the performance, you will have to do the exercise over another time.

Exercise IX

If you are doing this at home, your parent will try to give an actual party — such as your birthday party — during which you may do this exercise. Or you may invite some of your friends to join you during this particular session with your parent so that they may join in the fun.

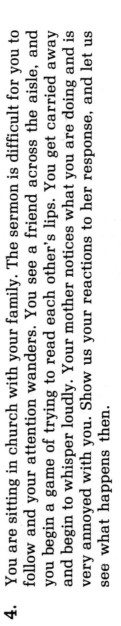

3. Your teacher has chosen you to make a poster which must be used in the assembly hall today. It is important that it be ready shortly, and there is no more paper so you are told to be extremely careful with the one piece you have received. While the teacher is busy elsewhere, you accidentally knock over the ink bottle, ruining the poster. Your teacher returns just as this occurs. Show us clearly your actions and reactions to the teacher's response.

4. You are sitting in church with your family. The sermon is difficult for you to follow and your attention wanders. You see a friend across the aisle, and you begin a game of trying to read each other's lips. You get carried away and begin to whisper loudly. Your mother notices what you are doing and is very annoyed with you. Show us your reactions to her response, and let us see what happens then.

Practice Project

Now here is our *Practice Project* which has been designed to help you further with communication and communion:

Practice Project. (1) Today I want you to use your awareness at home to observe your own actions and reactions with members of your own family. When you sit down to dinner, for example, you must be an observer of that dinnertime period. I want you to watch and listen to the dinner conversation. When other members of the family talk to one another, watch and listen and see how they react to each other. Try to get "inside" the situation and feel what they feel. If it is a pleasant conversation, try to understand what makes it so pleasant. If there should be an argument, try to decide what causes the argumentative responses — how does a remark made by one person cause the other person annoyance? How does the discussion end? How do you fit in? When someone speaks to you, what is it in that conversation that triggers your reaction of pleasure? Of anger? Of sadness?

(2) Now take another situation. Do you have a brother or sister (if you have none, think about one of your friends)? How do you get along with him/her? Can you share your games, books or records, for instance? Or do you sometimes have squabbles over your property or ideas? Do you have fights? Hit one another? What starts these? Try to be fair in observing one of these arguments — watch what's going on impartially — as if you were looking at someone else. It is hard, but you can do it. Who was it who started the argument? Why did you react as you did? Did your brother/sister/friend make you angry? How? If you had not answered

Practice Project

back with anger but had tried to remain calm, could you have avoided the argument? How? What could you have said instead that would have changed your brother/sister/friend's reaction? Think about everything that happens and try to see what makes it happen — how one person's action will cause the reaction of the other.

When you have your next session with your teacher or parent, tell about what you observed, what you have learned from your observations.

to a cooling.
air conditioned room. . .

You make an *adaptation*
when you come in out of
the summer heat. . .

or from a blizzard. . . .

to the comforting warmth of home.
FEEL the transition (change)
when you show
an adaptation onstage.
The audience will FEEL it too.

10. Adaptation

If your family suddenly moved to another city, you would find that you had to adapt or adjust yourself to your new home or apartment, your new school, your new friends — in fact you would even have to start over to make new friends. An *adaptation*, then, is really an adjustment or fitting in — changing to fit different conditions.

Onstage too we have *adaptations*. Here we consider an adaptation as the overcoming of a physical obstacle to our aim.

(a) Action = What do I do?
(b) Aim = Why do I do it?
(c) Adaptation = How do I do it?

Adaptation is particularly necessary in communion among actors on the stage. In order for one actor to adjust to another as the characters they portray, each must feel the other's presence there onstage, and each must be affected by the other's personality. Let me explain a bit more simply. In life we may know ahead of time what we wish to ask another person as well as why, but *how* we do it is another story — the *how* often comes unexpectedly. For example, you have an important appointment at 3 p.m. It is quarter to three and your teacher has decided to keep you after school. Now you must try to understand your teacher's circumstances before you can go to her with a good reason for leaving and thus avoiding detention. Since you want to be on time for your appointment, you must do all you can to avoid staying after school. Let's examine this situation for (a) action; (b) aim; (c) adaptation. You have the appointment — the teacher wishes you to remain after school. Her wish forms a block or obstacle to your aim. Therefore your understanding of her circumstances — why she wishes you to stay — requires you to create an adjustment to the situation in order to over-come her obstacle to your aim. There would be no obstacle if it weren't for your teacher's decision. If you can understand that you must adjust yourself with regard to the teacher's aim (either you will accept it or you will find a way to change it), then you will also understand that actors too must adjust to each other onstage in much the same way people adjust to accept change in life. Whenever they meet onstage, just as in private life, each person's behavior comes about because of his relationship with the other people around him.

If you talk to a two or three-year-old child, you will have to adjust your speech to his mentality and speak simply or he will not understand you.

If you talk to an important grownup, such as your school principal, you do not speak in the same way you speak to your playmates. You approach him with the respect due an older person and the head of your school.

If you want to ask your father to increase your allowance, you must first take measure of his mood, his appearance (is he extremely tired or does he seem rested? Does he appear discontented or happy?) and how busy he happens to be at the moment. You would not want to approach him to ask such a favor if you saw that he was in the middle of some work he'd brought home from the office. Would you ask for more allowance at a time when your father has just punished you for doing something wrong? All of these are obstacles which you must overcome before you can realize your aim of increased allowance. The way you would overcome these particular obstacles, of course, would be merely to wait for a better time to approach your father — a time when he would be likely to look upon your request more favorably.

Besides adapting to people around us, we also adjust to new conditions. When you step out of an air-conditioned room into the heat of summer outdoors, you are adapting. When night falls, you no longer behave as you did at noon or in the morning. You put on the lights; you do not play outdoors at night but stay in the house. At a certain time you take a bath and put on your bedclothes. You are adapting to the change in time — just as when you awake in the morning, you do not behave in the same way you did when you were tired and went to bed.

When you come inside after a sleigh ride in the middle of winter, you react differently to the atmosphere of your home than you did in midsummer when you came in to change out of your bathing suit into dry clothing. If you are given a difficult task to complete and you treat it more as a game than a job, there too you are adapting.

Exercise X. *How Do I Do It?*

Action = What do I do?
Aim or purpose = Why do I do it?
Adaptation or adjustment = How do I do it?

The following exercises will help you to see how your adaptation (How do I do it?) is a direct result of your action (What do I do?) and the aim or purpose of that action (Why do I do it?). Always remember that although the action and aim may be determined beforehand, the adaptation will depend upon your fellow actor's behavior as well as upon other obstacles you may discover in the course of your action onstage.

1. You want your mother to get you a special dress/suit for a birthday party. She is trying to save money for a vacation trip later in the year. Try to achieve your aim by the most effective means. Take time to build all the possible circumstances in which this could happen.

2. You were left alone in the house for a few minutes while your mother went outside to hang up the clothes. During that time you were examining the clock on the mantel and you dropped and broke it. Your mother has just come back into the house, and you want to avoid punishment, as you know you were forbidden to touch the clock. Since it is an heirloom and cannot

Exercise X

be replaced, you are worried. Make everything you imagine concrete and logical. Use all possible adaptations to achieve your aim.

3. You have been introduced to a new girl/boy who just moved into your apartment house/neighborhood. Show us your first meeting. Remember, he/she is the same age as you.

4. You have just met the new principal of your school. Show us this first meeting. Remember, he is an important person.

5. You have just come in out of a snowstorm. Show us your adaptation to the atmosphere indoors. Remember you will still feel the effects of the cold for a few minutes after you come in.

Here now is our *Practice Project* for next time:

Practice Project. All of your adaptations in everyday life will help you to adapt onstage. So for our *Practice Project* this time, I would like you to think about adaptation and try to pick out as many examples of adaptation — to people, to places, to changed conditions — as you can recognize in your own life.

Practice Project

Be ready to tell about these next time you come together with your teacher or parent to continue our work.

What kind of music is it?

When you move about the room with music think inwardly of its tempo-rhythm. . . .

11. Pacing Your Role with Tempo and Rhythm

Have you ever listened through a stethoscope to your own heartbeat? If you owned a stethescope you could find out something very interesting about your heartbeat. It changes with you. For instance, if you were jumping rope or playing softball and then listened to your heart, you would find it beating very fast and unevenly. But suppose you had been asleep for several hours before you listened to your heart. How do you think it would sound then? If you said much slower and steadier, you would be right. Your heart has tempo and rhythm.

Have you ever been outdoors when the rush hour traffic goes by? All the fathers are in a hurry to get home from work. If there is a delay and the cars are all stopped for a short time, you begin to hear the horns honking, showing the impatience of the drivers to be on their way. There is a tempo (speed) and rhythm (beat) here too. It is quite different from the slow traffic that went by earlier, isn't it?

Throughout every minute of life tempo and rhythm are constantly present, inside us as well as outside us. Everything that happens, moment by moment, in our lives occurs in a tempo-rhythm. You go off to school in the morning and come home that afternoon in different tempo-rhythms. You eat your school lunch in one tempo-rhythm but the lunch served at a party in another. As the waves in the ocean ebb and flow, so does the tempo-rhythm in and around us. When we are excited, our tempo-rhythm steps up — when we are calm and quiet, it slows down. That's what makes life so interesting. We would all be bored to tears if our tempo-rhythm remained constantly the same. Thank goodness it doesn't.

When you have done something remarkable — like winning a race or getting "A" on your report card — you have a different tempo-rhythm from when you have done something wrong and are feeling guilty about it. When you look at a beautiful sunset, your tempo-rhythm will be quite different from what it will be when you see something ugly. There is a correct tempo-rhythm, then, for everything you do. This is true on the stage too. Every action on the stage must be performed in the tempo-rhythm it would have in real life.

If you have the correct tempo-rhythm, it will help you to concentrate and keep you from being distracted or having your attention wander. It helps you when you work out the logic (reasoning) and proper arrangement of your actions. And it must fit in with the given circumstances of your scene. (The given circumstances include everything you know about the character and the play: the situation, time and place in which your scene is set.) For example, if you were in a fight scene, you could not move wearily or sluggishly if the scene called for you to be fighting hard. If you had a death scene to play, you would not use all your energy and brightness, would you? To keep the truth in your actions onstage, you must find the correct tempo-rhythm, for your actions cannot be truthful if they are too fast or too slow. Each scene has its own perfect pacing — timing and beat — and if you, the actor, wish to keep the audience's attention, you must find the correct tempo-rhythm for both the scene and the character you portray.

When you have the correct tempo-rhythm to help make your action truthful, it will stir your feelings so that you will be a better actor.

The building up of "struggles" in the role you are playing also influences the rhythmic pattern. The rhythm becomes different when the objects of a struggle change and different means are used in the struggle. To show you more clearly what I mean, let us take an example and examine it. If the character you portray is having a fist fight with an angry young man and the script calls for the sudden entrance of a policeman, your character's rhythm must change the very instant he observes the presence of the policeman. *How* it changes will be up to you as a creative actor. Is your character a bully — willing to fight a weaker person but afraid of authority? Is he the hero fighting for the good name of the heroine? If he is the hero, he will be glad to see the arrival of the policeman and surely will enlist his aid with his eyes and expression — even before he has any lines to speak to the policeman. If he is the bully, on the other hand, he will show his fear of the policeman before speaking. He may even stop fighting immediately and slink away.

Exercise XI. *Speed and Beat or Tempo-Rhythm*

In these exercises it might be helpful for you to clap or beat out with your hand or foot, in a rhythmical way, what you are experiencing inwardly.

1. You are finishing your homework. A TV program you particularly want to see will be on in ten minutes. Find the correct tempo-rhythm. Tap out the beat with hands or feet.

2. Your mother has asked you to make your bed and clean up your room. You have to do it, but you don't really feel like it. Show us the proper tempo-rhythm. Will you work fast, to get it over with, or will you dawdle, trying to draw it out? Show us by your beat.

3. Music is written to a particular beat — 4/4 or march time, 3/4 or waltz time, etc. Move about the room with music. Think inwardly of the tempo-rhythm you detect. This time do not beat them out. You have the music, and your audience can hear and tell the speed and beat. You just follow the tempo-rhythm of the music with your movements.

4. Walk in a funeral procession. (Clap your hands to show the tempo-rhythm, along with your walk.)

Practice Project

5. Walk on your way to school when you know you are going to be late. (Clap your hands to the proper tempo-rhythm.)

Here is your *Practice Project* for our next session:

Practice Project. At home try to discover the various tempo-rhythms that affect you as you go about your daily life. When you awake in the morning, try to feel the particular speed and beat of your actions. As you walk to school (or ride if you take a bus or car) notice the difference in speed and beat: (1) if you are on time and (2) if you are late. When you are playing after school, notice the tempo-rhythm within and without you: (1) if you are playing a quiet game like checkers, (2) if you are running a race and (3) if you are riding your bicycle. Tell in class (or to your parent if you are studying at home) what you found out about your own tempo-rhythms. Did you notice how they changed? How different they were from one another? Tell us about it next time.

Action and reaction—
one follows the other.

You discover a man threatening
your elderly employer
with a heavy andiron.
What will you do?

12. Discovering Meaning Through Actions

When you are given a part in a play, you are just one of the actors through whom the story of the play is presented to the audience. Nevertheless, your role must also project the main aim of the play.

It will be easier for you to discover the main aim of the play if you study the actions as they follow one another rather than trying to understand immediately the play as a whole. By studying the actions of the characters in the given circumstances of the play, you will be able to understand the whole meaning of the play.

We have already discussed given circumstances (see Chapter 11) The given circumstances include everything you know about the play:

1. The plot (plan or main story) of the play.
2. The period in history (era or century) in which the play takes place.
3. The time of the year, day or hour; and place of action.
4. Conditions of life of the characters. (Are they rich or poor?)
5. The director's and the actors' explanation of the play's meaning.
6. The scenery of the play.
7. The properties to be used by the actors during the play.
8. Lighting.
9. Sound effects.
10. Costumes.

What is your reason for being onstage? If you will remember you are there to communicate what you do and why you do it to your audience, it will help you.

Besides the play itself having a main aim or objective, each happening or group of happenings in the play has a main or central action as well as secondary actions. Let's take an example of an episode in a play and examine it now:

You are playing a character who is asked to stop an uneven fight between two friends. Your main action is to *stop the fight*. In the course of doing this you may have to *blame* one friend for starting the fight; you may encourage the other to stand up for his rights and refuse to be pushed around. By trying actively to carry out these purposes, which are actually the "adaptations" (means to achieve the aim) which we have discussed in a previous chapter, you give the whole episode meaning, variety and interest.

So you see if you are to understand what your action is at any given moment of the play, you must discover the meaning of each episode through actions. Actions must *always* be closely connected to the idea of the play. Every moment you are onstage, you must be striving to communicate the idea of the play through your actions. Actions speak louder than words, says an old proverb. If you complete your actions faithfully, you will involve your feelings or emotions, and they, in turn, will be communicated to your audience.

But you must determine the precise action for the specific episode. For instance, your first two specific actions in this scene where you stop a fight are to (1) rush over to the characters who are fighting and actually (2) *separate them*. Other actions then may include *taking* each one aside to talk with him privately, *accusing one of provoking the fight and encouraging the other to defend himself better.*

As you speak to each fellow actor, you, in the guise of your own character, will act in a way that is in agreement with the character you have already shown the audience in past scenes. You will be showing us by your actions as well, how you feel about each of the others. For example, your own actions toward the one who started it all will show annoyance — you might step towards him in a menacing attitude — while your behavior toward the other, who was losing the fight, will show concern. (You might put an arm around his shoulders.)

Deciding upon your actions in a given episode of the play, then, will give purpose to your character's behavior. So remember that for you to understand the actions, you will have to study the play, action by action. You will also have to know something about the period of time in which the play is set, and other external circumstances. You must also be able to understand what the playwright meant to say — what his aim was in writing the play. As an actor you must be able, too, to decide which particular actions would be most typical of the character you play and to use those actions in your part.

If you are going to do a school play, you will find a short discussion of the play will help to clarify all these points. Note to teacher or parent: Please see Guide at back of the book in this regard.

There is generally an obstacle — something that *opposes* the action. You, the actor, must discover those obstacles which your character must overcome. In the case of the character who had to stop the unequal fight between two others, the counteraction may be the reaction of the two characters to what he is trying to do for them. For instance, when he accuses the first of starting the unfair fight, that character may become belligerent (angry and warlike) and tell him to mind his own affairs or else receive a punch in the nose. And when he tries to give confidence to the second fellow, that character could be so frightened of his opponent that he might cringe and cower behind his benefactor or helper, trying to hide completely. Rather than taking courage from the interference, he might become even more cowardly. These, then, would be obstacles or counteractions for your character to overcome by his action. The overcoming of such obstacles makes you perform your action more vividly, with more strength and energy. Remember that each character in the play has his own main object of struggle — and it is how he meets his obstacles that shows the audience what kind of character he is.

Exercise XII. *Discovering Meaning Through Actions*

We will pretend the following are scenes from plays. Create the proper actions, and show us how your character overcomes his obstacles in each:

1. A beautiful princess who deeply loves her father, the king, must choose from among four suitors the one she wishes to marry. Each young man has a special gift to offer: One brings great wealth to her father's kingdom, the next has great powers of magic which he will use to thwart the king's enemies, the third can offer nothing but his love for he truly loves the princess, and the fourth brings political power through his own father's connections which can make the kingdom of the princess' father a world power. Show us how she reasons, what she feels, and whom she chooses. Make every action count.

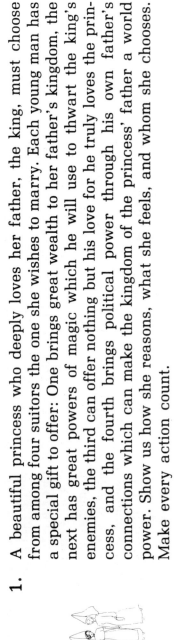

2. An old and powerful magician is dying. A young but cruel doctor has promised to save his life with a wonderful new drug he has discovered, but only if the magician teaches him all his secrets and promises never to practice magic again. What would you do if you were that magician? Show us by your inner and outer actions. (Let us see his age and condition clearly.)

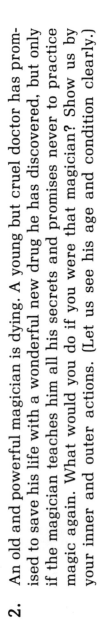

Exercise XII.

3. A teenager is taking an examination for a scholarship which means a lot to him as his parents are too poor to pay the college fees and the teenager cannot go to college if this scholarship falls through;

The room is full of students, all taking the exam. The teenager has reached a crucial (very important) question on the exam paper — one which carries 60 points — which he needs in order to pass. If he doesn't answer this question correctly, he will fail the exam. The supervising teacher is called out of the room for a few moments (leaving the students on their honor) . . . enough time for the teenager to cheat and copy from a neighbor's paper. The teenager is normally very honest, but there is a lot at stake here. What will he do? Will the other student allow him to copy from his paper? Will he try?

4. You are a middle-aged servant in the house of a wealthy landowner. You have been told by your employer, who is well on in years, that he has mentioned you in his will and at his death you are to receive a great deal of money. You come home one day to find a man threatening to murder your employer with a heavy andiron from the fireplace. What will you do? What action (if any) will you take? What will the counteraction of the would-be murderer be? How will you react then?

Practice Project

Even our *Practice Project* for this time will be a kind of review to help you to discover meaning through action.

Practice Project. For our project this time I would like you to read a play. Perhaps you have one in your English book, or perhaps your teacher has a play in mind for future production at school and will let you take it home now for study. If not, you can easily get a book of plays from the library. Pick out one play and read it at home.

After you have read it once, go through it again. This time I want you to find the main aim of the play by studying the actions in each episode. Now choose a part you would like to play, and go through all that character's lines, trying to form an idea of the character's main object of struggle in the play. Scene by scene, go over in your mind your character's proper actions in the given circumstances.

When you next meet with your teacher or parent, be prepared to tell the story of the play and its main aim. Give some examples of your character's actions, and show how he or she might overcome the obstacles (counteractions) in a particular scene.

The lion tamer is suddenly
in real danger. . . .

but his audience must not suspect.
Have you used the LIFELINE
of your play and your character?

13. The Super-Objective and the Through Line of Action (Lifeline)

When an author writes a play, he has a reason for doing so. He wants to get a particular idea across to his audiences. It is this *main idea* of the play that we, as actors, must carry to the spectators. This is true of a school play you perform for your friends, just as much as it is true on Broadway. When you have a part in any play, it is your job, as well as the director's or teacher's), to transmit to the audience what the playwright had in mind when he wrote his play: his main idea. Stanislavski called this main idea the *super-objective* and taught that the super-objective should be the final goal of every performance. So strive to show the play's main idea in everything you do onstage.

When you, the actor, are preparing your role, you must have the main idea clear in your mind from the beginning, and it must remain clear to you until the end of the play. It will help you to clarify the super-objective of any play you are working on if you will give this main idea an expressive name. For instance, the super-objective (main idea) of *Beauty and the Beast* is that kindness and the beauty of goodness can overcome evil or ugliness. So you might call the super-objective here "beauty overcomes ugliness," or "good overcomes evil."

If you forget the super-objective, you will break the "lifeline" of the play. The line of life which runs through the play must not be broken or the play will be ruined. So always keep the super-objective in mind when you appear in a class play. The super-objective regulates the character's logical (reasonable) actions, making the meaning of the play come to life for the audience. The life of the play is what makes a play seem *real* to spectators while they are watching it.

When you have decided what the super-objective of your play is, you have strengthened the "lifeline" of the play. Let us now turn to the "lifeline" of your character within the play. For an actor's part to seem logical and to fit properly with the rest of the play, he should mentally trace a line which will run through his own role throughout the play. This imaginary line is what Stanislavski called "the through line of action." This is how you actively put to use the main idea which you have already found in the play . . . and if you use your "through line of action," it will help coordinate or unite the separate parts of your role into a well-organized whole.

Remember, as an actor, working on a part, you must continually check your *through line of action* to make sure you have the right activity, order, logic, color and contrast in your role — and that all these things work together properly to project the super-objective or main idea of the play. All your actions in the play, then, must be guided by the through line of action. To be in their proper order and to be logical, every action must depend upon the *previous action* as well as on the *following* one. This is what the through line of action is in simple terms: all of your character's actions interwoven logically with the purpose of expressing the main idea. Besides the super-objective or main idea of the play as a whole, each character has his own basic or main purpose in the given circumstances of the play, his own most important struggle. You can see therefore that the character's aim throughout his role is his own super-objective and through line of action. It is what *makes* the character move, his reason for being. Now the goal toward which your character struggles in any given scene, act or episode of the play is called the *action* of that scene, act or episode. To make your character live on-stage, you must first find his super-objective. As you know, every play must have conflict or struggle, and this conflict in a play is created by the through line of action and the struggle or counteraction of the various characters in the play.

If you truly try to fulfill the actions leading to the super-objective of your role, you will find it gives you inspiration for, understanding of and insight into (a way of "looking into") your character.

The super-objective and through line of action should be found not only in your roles on-stage but also whenever you perform an exercise for your teacher or parent. If you try to find them each time, you will soon see how much better your performances will be.

Exercise XIII. *Super-Objective and Through Line of Action*

Find the super-objective and through line of action for each of the following episodes:

1. You are a lion trainer with the circus. One of the lions suddenly turns vicious and attacks you. You have a chair and a whip, and it is your job to keep all the lions in line. However, when the one began to growl and grow angry, he inflamed the others, and now you have to fight off the main animal while also keeping the others at bay. You must calm them down and get out of the cage — but at the same time you are performing for an audience and must keep them interested and unaware that you are in real danger.

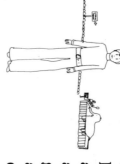

2. You have gone to a zoo in another town with your teacher and class. While you were in the monkey house, you became so interested in the antics of two of the monkeys that you didn't see the class leave the building, and apparently they didn't miss you. When you were finally ready to leave, you couldn't find your class anywhere. You have no money with you, and you don't know how to get back home from this strange town. It is beginning to get dark.

112

3. You are playing with a friend in the back yard. You get into an argument over a game, and he picks up a stone and throws it at you. You duck, so you are not hit, but you are so angry you throw a stone at him. It hits him just above the eye, and he falls down, bleeding and apparently unconscious. You rush to him and try to revive him, but he won't wake up. You know you must get help, but you are afraid to tell anyone what you have done. Because he remains unconscious, you recognize how urgent it is to hurry.

4. Your mother had to go out on an errand. You are alone in the house when the phone rings. You answer it. It is the hospital, telling you that your mother has been in an accident. It is up to you to contact your father at work, but you are so upset you cannot remember his phone number, although you do know the name of his company and where it is located. You must reach your father so that both of you can go to the hospital immediately.

5. You are helping your teacher by arranging the room for a class party for Hallowe'en. You have placed plastic skeletons, jack-o-lanterns and creepy

bugs around the room when a boy comes in with a real, live spider. You are frightened of bugs and try to get him to take it away, but before you succeed, the rest of the class comes in and the party begins. The boy has placed the spider on the teacher's chair, and the teacher is approaching her desk.

Practice Project. What's your favorite story? A *Wrinkle in Time, Gulliver's Travels, Pippi Longstocking, Homer Price,* or maybe *My Side of the Mountain* or even the old favorite, *Mary Poppins?* Whatever it is, I want you to think about it at home before your next lesson. See if you can't visualize it as a play. Think about what the author was trying to say in his story. What was his main idea (his super-objective)? Then think about the main character in the story. How does that character make the story move and live? What is his special "through line of action" leading to the successful conclusion of the story? Next time you meet with your teacher or parent, tell what you have discovered about the super-objective. About the main character's "through line of action." This will give you added experience and help you to find the main idea and through line of action in the plays you will be using in school.

You are a princess
at a formal state party,
where you wear
an ermine robe and a crown.
You stand in a receiving
line to greet the guests.

Show us the scene,
without any actual props.

14. The "Watcher Within"

If you want to become a really good actor, you will have to develop a sort of sixth sense: a watcher inside yourself who takes note of everything you do outwardly for your characterization. The smallest movement onstage — a turn of the head, a change in the direction of a look — can tell the audience something about the inner feelings of your character and project his thoughts. But your performance does not depend upon the character's inner life alone but also on the bodily movements and voice of the character which *show* these inner thoughts.

When a musician plays his instrument, he transmits feelings to his audience. Your own body and voice constitute your instrument when you are an actor. Actions of the body and voice are your music. To use your instrument perfectly, it must be tuned — or prepared for use — just as a piano or a violin is tuned. This is one reason I have been giving you *Exercises* and *Practice Projects* in every chapter of this book — to help you prepare your own instrument for use on the stage.

We have been working on bodily movements as well as the use of your voice in creating a character. We've been "tuning" you up; and by now you must be familiar with all the ways an actor can use his body and his voice to his best advantage.

You must know by now, then, that it would be very wearing and tiresome to the audience to have to listen to an actor whose speech is not correct and under-standable. An actor cannot afford to have speech defects, nor can he talk in a sloppy fashion if he expects the audience to hear and understand him. When you learned to read in school, you learned also to speak proper English (or you were meant to). Naturally, there may be a time when you will have to play a character who doesn't speak perfect English or use good grammar — or even one who has a speech defect such as a lisp or a stutter — but that is no excuse for you to speak sloppily or incoherently (confusedly) onstage. You still must be heard and understood, and therefore, when you speak in the words of the character, you must remember to speak loudly enough to be heard (but do not shout) and clearly enough to be understood.

This book is not the place for a long discussion on voice production and placement or the use of the diaphragm (the muscular partition that separates the chest cavity from that of the abdomen) in breathing and projecting your voice. It would take a book in itself. Your English teacher or, if your school has one, your speech teacher will undoubtedly work on these things. However, I do want to caution you here to make the best of your voice onstage. When an actor breathes properly and has good, clear diction and a well-placed voice (not nasal or "breathy"), he will not find himself *forcing* but will be able instead to speak naturally and either loudly (as in the case of a shout) or softly (as in a stage whisper) and still be heard in the top row of the balcony.

Stage Fright

Some of the greatest actors in the world have confided to friends that even after years in their profession they still get stage fright before a performance. However, as they do not let it get the "upper hand," it generally goes away the minute they are onstage saying their first line of the play.

Tenseness of the muscles, the reaction to an audience, can interfere with — inhibit or hold back — your natural physical actions onstage and thus also interfere with your correct inner feelings and inner experience. This tension of the muscles can paralyze you on the stage if you let it. However, if you keep your "watcher within" at the ready, this cannot happen. This "observer" within yourself — who is always alert and will instantly find the place of un-necessary tension and quickly get rid of it — will work for you as long as you trust that it will. Here is how it is done: First, remember Stanislavski's constant caution, "Never do things in general — always be specific." Concentrate on a specific thought and a definite action, and it will help you to relax and lose your self-consciousness immediately.

Your body is as important onstage as your voice. Therefore you should train yourself to stand, sit, walk and move gracefully, with good posture at all times (unless of course the char-acterization calls for poor posture and awkward gestures). Stanislavski himself wanted his actors to improve their posture and learn to make their movements graceful. However, you must always move in character, and if your role calls for you to have poor posture, your posture must not be perfect or you'll of course be out of character. The same holds true of voice and speech.

It is only common sense to realize that if your character never went to school, cannot read or write and thus does not use good grammar, you must not correct his grammatical errors. But "making graceful movements" — whether of voice or body — does not mean the actor should use mannerisms or mechanical gestures or try to be "cute" onstage. An actor must never pose — he must be. Neither should you choose any gesture for your character merely because it is graceful. Always remember that the gesture must be the outward form of an inner experience. Then, and only then, will it have purpose and be logical and truthful for the character. The body and voice should be trained so that they are able to show outwardly the inner experiences. But as an actor you must also train your inner tools so that both may grow together in experience.

In other words, you are using your MAGIC IF and your outer actions both together, as we have discussed in earlier chapters. They work hand-in-hand — the inner (thought) and outward (action). Therefore, while the inner technique or method of performance helps your ability to create the proper feelings, the physical or bodily technique will make your body responsive to the inner impulse (push or tendency to act) and train your feeling of truth and proper form to have an "insight" of its own — to be trustworthy.

If you had been a student studying under the great Stanislavski, you would have had to work a great deal on rhythm, gesture, acrobatics, diction, voice, expressive word and historical ceremonies. You would have found that he considered it very important for an actor to control his voice and bodily movements and to "know how to wear a costume."

When you play a part on the stage, you are actually creating a new being. This new person must have the correct costume and movement. The moment of donning the costume can work a kind of "magic" in helping to change you into the character you play You must familiarize yourself with everything your character knows, especially with his clothing, and you must, if he does, know how to use all the accessories that go with the costume — such as a crown, a poncho, a gun, a wig, a banjo, a knife or even a wheelchair, if your character uses one.

Every form of expression you use in creating your character must be specific, definite, clear and simply done. All movements, gestures and cadences (rises and falls) of speech must be precise and clear as well. You will be able to perform truthfully, naturally, in your physical action only if you practice with your body and voice the proper movements for your character and the proper vocal intonations (manner of sounding words or speaking) and inflections (change in the tone or pitch). Only then will you truly live the experiences of the character you play while you are onstage.

A good performance depends upon the joining or uniting of the character's inner feelings with his expressive action (or the outward expression of his inner feelings).

Exercise XIV. *Posture and Speech*

1. You are a prince (princess) at a formal state party where you wear an ermine robe and a crown and stand in a receiving line greeting the guests. Using these given circumstances, create the scene, using the proper posture and speech for the character.

2. You are an elderly, tired beggar, wearing rags and tatters. You are standing in a breadline waiting your turn to receive free food. Let us see the character and hear him as he talks with his neighbors on the line. (What time of year is it? What time of day?)

3. You are a criminal being chased by a policeman. You have just robbed a bank, and the policeman has followed you to your hideout. You come inside, out of breath from the chase, but quickly hide the "loot" and station yourself at one of the windows with a gun. The policeman calls to you to give yourself up. You answer him through the window. Make the scene live. What will be your posture and speech here? (GIRLS: There are lady criminals!)

4. You are a baby, crawling about in its playpen. Your mother comes into the room and stops to play with you. The only word you know is "mama."

Exercise XIV.

5. You are a very old woman crippled by arthritis, walking with the help of a cane. You enter a store, find what you want on the shelf, and take it — wearily — to the counterman to be wrapped. As he collects your money and wraps your package, the two of you get into a short conversation.

6. You are a young bride (groom) coming out of the church after the wedding ceremony with your new husband (wife). You have a chance to speak together briefly before the guests come out to congratulate you and throw rice. Think about what sort of person you are. What is your station in life? How happy do you feel? (Was the wedding your own choice — or was it "arranged" by parents, etc.?) Your feelings always affect your posture and speech. Let us "see" the scene.

Our *Practice Project* this time will give you some much needed experience in the art of "costume."

Practice Project. Today I want you to borrow some old clothes from your mother (if you are a girl) or father (if you're a boy). Consider them as a costume for a play in which you portray your parent. Put on the costume, and when you are dressed, walk, move about, sit, stand and behave as though you were your mother or father — remembering their habits, actions,

Practice Project

manner, etc. (If the clothing is much too large for you, you will have to pin or tuck it up to fit you.) Wear the clothes until you feel comfortable in them, as though they belonged to you and you wore them or similar things all the time. But at the same time keep your "watcher within" alert, and be able to observe what you are doing. Next time tell us about it. How did it feel to play the part of your mother (father)? Did you remember your MAGIC IF? Did it help you to behave "as if" you were your parent?

You are a moth.
flying around an outdoor lamp.
The flickering light
fascinates you.

. . .Let YourSELF go!

15. Creating the Character

"Genius is an actor who sees life and is able to recreate it on the stage."
— Stanislavski

We have been talking throughout this book about the various elements of the Stanislavski system. Now we shall try to put them all together as we work on creating a character. Let us see how well you have listened and worked, how much you got from your *Exercises* and *Practice Projects*. You should by now be ready to use all you have learned in preparing a characterization for a school play.

You know that each of the arts has a special means of expression. Writers use words. musicians use sounds, painters use colors — but the actor uses *human action*. The audience can know only what the actor tells them by his words and actions. Just as we know about people in our own lives by seeing their physical actions and hearing what they say (and we know that what they say and do is really the result of their particular aims at a given time), so it is on the stage.

A stage action explains to the audience what the character is doing at a given moment and why he is doing it. All the character's inner aims are expressed by bodily actions, and every physical or bodily movement has an aim behind it. (Even if it is not immediately apparent, you will remember how we learned to "read between the lines of life" on the stage.)

If you remember that the bodily action and the inner aim of the character you portray reflect one another, you will understand the basic idea of the Stanislavski system of acting. Movements show the person's interests, tastes, habits, moods, feelings. The inner life of the person is always expressed through a simple physical action. If we see the logic of the person's physical movements, it will also give us an understanding of his inner feelings. You show what you mean by your bodily actions — these actions in turn tell the audience, by their logic, what is in your mind at the time. So it is clear that unless you think the inner thoughts of the character when you are onstage, these inner thoughts cannot come through to your audience, since your physical actions can only reflect what is in your mind. Thus without both the inner and outer life of your character, you cannot create a true person on the stage — one who seems real to your audience. There are actors, for instance, who merely "rest", while another actor is talking and just wait for the cue to tell them it is time to speak or move again. This is wrong. This is not creating a *living character*. To create a living character onstage as in real life, you must follow the laws of nature — live both inwardly and outwardly.

To do this, you must realize it is very important for you to see the character you play in terms of his actions. While you are onstage, you must build the life of a completely new human being — his body and his spirit. Therefore, every moment he is onstage, this new person must use actions which will express that life completely. And once you realize that a person is always being (living what he is) and becoming (growing into what his potential means him to be), you will then realize that no character you create can possibly be dull.

The *creative* part of your work as an actor, therefore, is your choice of correct actions. Anything you do onstage must reflect the character's complete life — so you know it is right if it helps to express your character's aims. If it does not express or reflect your character's inner thoughts and feelings, the action is wrong and you must choose another, during re-hearsals, to find the right movement.

Often the director (or as in this book, teacher or parent) can give you helpful suggestions for an action that seems right for your character — but the main job of finding these actions is yours, as the actor portraying that character. Let us say you are playing a very poor little child of about six or seven years old who has never had any toys to play with and suddenly receives a toy. As the actor showing that poor child to the audience, your choice of actions will be very important. If you show him playing with the toy as though he were quite used to handling it, you will not be showing truth on the stage. Instead, you must realize and show to your audience, *through your actions as the child*, that he has *never seen* such a toy before and thus does not even know the first thing about *handling* it, much less *playing* with it. You must be so awkward with that toy that your audience can see you have never owned such a thing before.

Now let's talk about creating strange or unusual characters — characters that are not human beings at all. Shakespeare had some strange creatures in his plays, such as ghosts or creatures like "Ariel" — a wraithlike figure who stands for an *idea*. (Ariel is an airy spirit in *The Tempest*.) In school you may have to play characters that are not human, such as animals or inanimate objects, in *allegorical* plays (plays that speak in symbols and sometimes use people to represent ideas). This is quite a challenge to your imagination. You must first decide how you think the idea of, let us say, love or hate would act if it had become embodied in a personality. How do you think an animal would behave if it were suddenly endowed with human qualities, such as speech and human action? It is great fun to play parts like these, as it gives you a chance *really* to use your imagination fully. You will find yourself thinking about things you may never have considered before, such as the knowledge that action does not always have to be movement and that sometimes the proper choice of action onstage will be, for that moment, *inaction* (no action). You may have to play a scene some time in which your character chooses to react to an obstacle by complete stillness — no action at all. That, too, will be action for your character, since it is his choice of what to do. He will have chosen to do nothing in this case. The Stanislavski system will help you just as much if you use it to create these imaginary creatures in school plays as it will when you play human parts.

Using all the things you have learned about the system — including the MAGIC IF, circles of attention, awareness and imagination, the action of voice and body, the memory of feelings, concentration, truth on the stage, communication etc. (in other words, *all* the elements of the system) — try to perform the following exercises, changing into the imaginary characters called for. Make your audience see what you are, feel what you feel and understand through what you do or do not do what it is you are and want.

Exercise XV. *Creating Strange Characters*

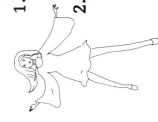

1. Be a stone. The rain is falling on you. Remember, a stone cannot walk, but show us by the use of your imagination what you would do if you could.

2. You are a weeping willow tree. Your branches are wide and hang low toward the ground. It is a sunny day and you are enjoying the weather, relaxing in the sun's warmth. You speak to your neighboring tree in the play.

3. You are a traffic light on a busy street. You cannot move away, but your lights constantly change color to direct the traffic. Automobiles are moving below you.

4. You are a carrot, growing in the garden among others of your kind. Can you communicate with them? Only your leaves reach above ground. It hasn't rained for some time . . . you are thirsty.

5. You are a lion, the King of the Jungle. A pesky monkey insists upon chattering in the tree just above your head while you are trying to take your afternoon nap.

Exercise XV.

6. You are a moth, flying around an outdoor lamp. The flickering light fascinates you, and you want to get closer to it.

There are many classic books written for young children which have been adapted for the stage. Alice in Wonderland has been performed as a play many times for movies, TV, stage, etc. Alice has many characters that are not real people — the Mad Hatter, the March Hare, the Playing Card People, Tweedledum and Tweedledee, the Cheshire Cat, and many others. In the book The Wind in the Willows, by Kenneth Grahame, which has also been dramatized, there is a Mole, a Water Rat, a Frog, a Badger and other small furry animals who speak and act as people. If you were putting on a play for younger children, you might have to perform similar parts, so the exercises you have just been working on should be of great value to you. You will note that in all the exercises above you have a definite purpose. Any action on the stage must have a purpose behind it. If it does not, it will just draw the audience's attention away from the meaning of the play.

Whether you play imaginary, animal or vegetable characters or real human beings in your school plays, you must remember that the purpose or aim is what determines the action . . . and the purpose must express individual life. For an action to be truthful on the stage, you, the actor, must be able to answer these questions: "Who am I?" "Where is the action occurring?" "With whom?" "What for?" You must know the given circumstances — everything the author has told you about the play and its action and characters. You are

Exercise XV.

ready to play your part when you know *what* the character does each moment he is onstage and *why* he does it. The actions you choose make the person real for the audience — his spirit as well as his body — and they must fit the overall purpose of the play (remember the "through line of action") and give the audience an understanding of the character's appearance, moods, habits, beliefs, tastes, and what he is striving for in the course of the play.

A painter recreates life on his canvas with paint. A writer recreates life in print. An actor recreates life by his movements and words on the stage. An actor must make a whole new being live — his habits as well as his feelings — and we know that each person in this world is an individual and different from every other human being in some ways, even though he may have some things in common with his fellow man. He is different and individual in the way he *approaches* a problem.

If there were three people sitting in an overly warm room and they all wanted some fresh air, each one would open the window differently. This is because each person has a different background, different interests in life, a different way of looking at things. Even within the same family each family member is different, depending upon whether he was born first, last or between several other children. How many other children there are in the family also affects a child's character. An only child will be quite different from a child brought up in a large family. A boy with only a brother will be different from a boy who has a sister, and both will differ from one with two sisters and a brother.

Every action of a person's inner life, every action and reaction to what goes on around

133

Exercise XV.

him, carries his own special one-of-a-kind stamp. So when you play a specific character on the stage, you must first learn everything you can about him — and what the author does not tell you, you must fill in for yourself: his past life, his personal interests, his aims and ambitions in life as well as his aims or purposes in the play. And you must also know what his hopes are for the future. Only then will you have created a fully rounded character rather than a one-dimensional, fictional being.

If all creatures on this earth have one thing in common, it is their individuality. If you have had pets at home, you will know what I mean. Just as it is with people, one cat or dog behaves quite differently from another. I once had a cat who constantly wanted to be petted and would snuggle up to anyone with that aim in mind. Then I had another cat who didn't care to be petted at all. She just wanted to go about her own business and be left alone. If you tried to pet her, she would nip you, playfully at first to show she didn't want to be bothered, but if you persisted, she would really get nasty and give you a definite nip to show she meant business before running off to be by herself. Now I have a dog who was guaranteed to be a good watchdog — but he loves people so much and makes friends so easily that he could never be a watchdog. It's all a matter of action and reaction, as you can see. So, when you play a part, you must create that special, individual *difference* — or logic behind your character's actions which is uniquely his own and no one else's. Plays that have had long runs on Broadway and have had a succession of different actors in the leading roles are good examples of the uniqueness that the actor brings to his performance. Sometimes someone who has been to the

Practice Project

same play twice, each time with a different actor in the leading part, has come away each time with a different reaction to or feeling about the play. It can seem like an entirely different play when a new actor creates the same role someone else has played for awhile.

Therefore, let us talk some more about creating your own specific character. To find his correct actions and reactions, you must first study the play. Find out everything the author intended him to be, and then carry it a step further by preparing in your own mind (or on paper if it helps you) an autobiography or life story of your character. When you have him thus set in time and place in his own special world, you must use your own ability to choose the actions which will be most typical of your character. Stanislavski told us that in characterizations we must first know the logic of actions in a play and then be able to put them all on one thread (through line of action) in a proper consecutive (one following the other) order. To find the proper consecutive order, all you need know is that all the actions must lead to the fulfillment of the main idea (super-objective) of the play and the role you perform.

Now here is a *Practice Project* that will help you do this on your own.

Practice Project. Here is something which at first glance may seem difficult, but it will be simple and fun for you with all the background you have by now absorbed. You are almost at the end of your present studies, and you must have noticed how much simpler each lesson becomes once you have mastered the earlier work. Prepare this at home, then, and be ready with it next time you meet with your teacher or parent.

Practice Project

Pretend you, yourself, are a character in a play. There is nobody you know better than yourself — so you can treat yourself as a character in a play about your own life. Take a pencil and paper and write down everything you know about yourself — from your earliest memories to the present. Then think about what you want for the future.

What do you want to become when you grow up? Write everything down and bring it in to read aloud to the class or your parent next time.

There is a bonus in this exercise, since it will help you to understand yourself better, while at the same time it will give your parent or teacher an opportunity to know more about you. The more we know about ourselves and others, the more we can work together harmoniously. See if you don't notice a difference in your real-life "harmonies" after this *Practice Project*. If you enjoy the results, you can adapt this project — you can use it as a "game" at one of your parties. You will find how helpful it is in getting to know your friends better when they, too, discover and tell you as much about themselves as they can.

No part is a small part.
What would you do if you were
the weeping willow tree in Exercise XV?
If you're not sure yet,
you need MORE WORK ON THE PART!

16. More Work on the Part

The *through line of action* leading to the super-objective (main idea) of the character's role in the play helps you to get a well-rounded characterization in relation to the other characters in the play. Following your continuous line of actions will make your part "fit in" properly and give it color and variety too. If you follow this imaginary line throughout the play, you will find your part fitting in harmoniously with the rest of the play, and your role will grow logically to its proper conclusion.

When you build your character's traits and behavior, remember that these should be made up of small, concrete, logical actions. For instance, you might show shyness by a gentle smile and a quick ducking down of the head — but it must suit your character and fit in with his other habits and traits. Or it might show, by contrast, that he is at odds with himself. And each action must be consecutive (follow in its proper order), must have the proper tempo-rhythm. (If you'd like a reminder about *tempo-rhythm*, turn back to Chapter Eleven.) Remember also to use your *concentration*. You must use as much concentration for each action as that action would require in real life. It is only through your ability to perform truthful physical actions onstage that you will find the inner world of your character. And when you have both inner and outer action, your character will live onstage, and your audience will follow his life with interest.

Now let's talk about your character's speech. The words he uses are chosen by the play-wright, but the *way* he says them will be your responsibility. You cannot say one word on the stage without first thinking and forming an image in your mind — just as you do in real life. So you must listen — *really listen* — to the other actors who speak to you onstage, and you must let yourself think and have mental images of what is being said before you reply. In other words you must allow your character to react to the other characters in the play. Stanislavski called the meaning behind the words, the subtext (or the meaning under the words). To him the subtext was the "inward life of a human spirit" which con-stantly flows under the words of a role. The subtext is to speech onstage what the through line of action is to action. Words too are part of a given moment in the play, and words are the results of thoughts and mental images.

Words are the most precious of your physical actions, since they have the power to create images in your fellow actors and these images have the power to stir their emotions — to make them laugh, cry, frown, smile, etc. Words carry feelings from one actor to another. At the same time they carry the action of the play forward so that the spectators are mentally and emotionally moving forward with the progress of the play.

"To speak means to act," Stanislavski told us, and when we listen to others speak, we hear and then visualize what we heard. In the process of trying to influence your fellow actors by your speech, you project to your audience the character you are playing. Though we must be careful to use good diction (to speak plainly and clearly) onstage, when the audience has difficulty understanding what the actor is saying, it may not necessarily be his diction that is at fault. It is more often the lack of true *communication* to the audience through the *communion* of the actors. So as your work on your role progresses and when you rehearse with your fellow actors, always be sure to create a true *communion* — as in life. Do not merely say lines to them. And in the same way, always listen when your fellow actor speaks to you, even if it is a repeat performance. Listen with "new ears" each time you rehearse or perform.

Do not forget either, as you work on a characterization, that you must first be sure you understand the aim or main idea of the play and then your own part of the action. You must prepare your own action in clear detail, with the knowledge that everything you do or say, think or feel must further the action of the play towards that main idea. So do not rush when you prepare your characterization. Take your time, and find out exactly what your purpose should be in order to further the play's main idea. Your teacher or director will no doubt take time to discuss the main idea of the play before giving out the parts, but whether she does or not, you must remember to do the work yourself. Find out for yourself the main idea of the play and just how your character takes part in achieving that aim.

Treat your character as a living person, and you cannot help but create a live human being on the stage. And even though the character was originally created by the playwright, you, as the actor, must recreate the character using your own ideas in *addition* to those hints and remarks the playwright has given about that character. In this way, when your own thoughts and ideas are joined to those of the playwright, you will create a whole new person for the stage. And in each play in which you have a part, you will be able to create another new person if you have used all your powers of perception to know your own inner world and the larger world about you. What a wonderful world of discovery opens to you when you become an actor — even if it is only once or twice a term when you appear in your class plays.

This method of using the playwright's character, but adding to it part of yourself — your own ideas and thoughts about that personality — is very important if you hope to create a living character onstage. Stanislavski used to say an actor must "go from himself", and yet not forget his own self — his own personal "I." You must do what might at first seem impossible: You must become another person while still remaining yourself. However, if you have been following all the elements of Stanislavski's famous system of acting as described in this book, you will know that this going from yourself while remaining yourself is not at all impossible. As a matter of fact, it is the logical end of all our work so far. Using your own MAGIC IF and all the other parts of our system, you find it quite natural now to be both the character and yourself at the same time. The "Watcher Within" remains the part of yourself which keeps track of everything you do as the character; he helps you to realize when your actions are right for the character as well as when they are wrong. When, for example, you are building the logical actions for your character (what would I do if?), you yourself must first find what is usual in such a situation — what your reactions would have in common with the reactions of other human beings — and *then* find the special individual traits and actions which make your character unusual or unique.

You must learn to build or create many different characters for different plays, discovering the essential habits and behavior of such characters while still remaining yourself — the *watcher within* who seeks for what is true and sincere on the stage.

And do not forget what we said earlier about building the character: You, the actor, must gather together all possible details and character traits — finding some of these in your memory of past experience, taking others from life around you. Stop, look and listen all the time in your daily life if you want to find the material you can later use for acting. Alertness, awareness and imagination are the basic traits needed by anyone who wants to do any acting. Study the people you know and even the passers-by in the street for impressions you may use on the stage. But later, when you start to use these in building a character, you must use only details that help to make your character an individual — a *specific* person. Remember also that *too many details* may tend to confuse the audience. A single external (outward) movement which is characteristic — distinguishing or showing the differences — of the personality of the person you are portraying is more impressive than a whole group of unnecessary motions. Your special attitude, your speech, your clothing, your every movement onstage must be characteristic of the person you are playing — and it is wise to remember the value of contrast too in planning your character's actions. Stanislavski told his actors, "When you play a nasty man, search for what is good in him." Not even the worst villain is always bad. And the use of different sides of a character, such as pointing up one of the villain's good traits, can make the portrayal of the nasty side of the man even stronger by contrast.

Lastly, let me point out that the audience itself is very important to you as you play your part up there on the stage. So keep that *watcher* within alert for audience reaction. For it is from hearing and sensing their reactions to what you are doing that you will know a great deal about whether your performance is right or wrong. Often the reaction of the audience can show an actor some point where he can improve his characterization. This is particularly helpful if there are to be two or three performances of the play. Next time you can try for a different audience response. So keep the *watcher* within at work so that you will know where you may improve your performance.

In cases where you will be performing your school plays for several audiences — let us say for two or three different assemblies at school and perhaps for a P.T.A. program as well — try to remember the Stanislavski slogan, "TODAY, HERE, NOW." It will make every performance a new experience. Each time you appear in the same role, if you try not to merely repeat yesterday's performance but to create each time a new true-life happening on the stage, your acting will always be fresh and neither your audiences, fellow actors nor you yourself will ever be bored.

Stanislavski insisted his actors have a creative attitude toward each performance. He had his cast arrive at the theatre in time to put on their makeup and costumes without rushing and to go over the important points of their roles before the performance began.

Take a look at the stage before it is time for your entrance — before the play begins. It will help you feel more at home with the setting of the play and the various objects on the stage where you will shortly be moving about.

Before you set foot onstage, you should know the whole day's activities of the character you play and what might have happened to him before he appears.

You should start playing your part a few minutes before you go on and proceed gradually and logically to the moment of your entrance.

You should think only of one action at a time. Your knowledge of the circles of attention will help you there.

The Exercises and the Practice Projects are over. If you have followed the instructions in this book carefully, you have done your groundwork. Now you are ready to appear in that play. Good luck to you!

There is one more thing to think about, however. Whether you're tired, upset by happenings at home or at school or not feeling up to par on the day of the performance, you will have to remember your own, personal MAGIC IF and act "as if" everything were perfect. You must put aside all personal problems and create a new being on the stage. When you are in the theatre — sick or well, tired or energetic — you concentrate on the play, and you perform.

"The show must go on" is a famous saying of theatre people, and now you are one of them — ready to create a whole new person out of the playwright's dream, your inner and outer experience, the MAGIC IF and your own, unique intelligence. GO TO IT!

Parent/Teacher Guide: Notes on the Exercises and Practice Projects

Parents and teachers are ideally suited to "direct" children in the Stanislavski system of acting. As parents and teachers our ultimate function is good leadership. Our children are primarily in need of guidance in the art of living — and specifically in each field they enter it is our job to head them in the proper direction. To do this, we need two vital elements: knowing the goal and superintending their aim towards it.

Along the way they must make mistakes and it is our job to train their awareness and imagination to recognize the errors and correct them. They cannot learn *if we do it for them*. We must only show the way so that they may develop self confidence. Our children will go on, with our encouragement, correcting each mistake as it occurs, if we give them the confidence that eventually the goal will be reached.

In this Stanislavski training, your pupils would progress even if they were to work completely on their own, but the speed and extent of their progress, working with you, will be in direct ratio to your encouragement and guidance.

If you will go over the book yourself, before the child begins to read it on his own, you will get some idea of the scope of the work. Teachers may prefer to have the students read the chapters aloud in oral reading sessions rather than at home. In such case, the Exercises in each chapter may follow naturally at the same session. However, please keep in mind that the *Practice Projects* are given at the end of each chapter since they are actually homework assignments. Therefore, it would be best to have the child perform for you his improvisations, etc. from the previously given *Practice Project* at the following session, while it is still fresh in his mind, before beginning the new work for that session.

You don't have to be an expert to direct your child in this work. Because of the character of audience reaction per se and the fact that your participation will be primarily that of audience to the child's actor, your own "watcher within" or instinct will tell you unerringly when and if the student has not succeeded. However, I have found the child takes to these studies naturally and there is little chance that he will not get his meaning across to you in any of these Exercises or *Practice Projects*. Merely on the assumption that there are exceptions, and that your pupil *could* be one of them, I have included herein methods you may use to help the student overcome any problems he may encounter. If in any of the Exercises he is not using both inner and outer actions in harmony, it will be obvious, since you will not feel what the Exercise is meant to convey. In such cases merely have him take a few minutes to concentrate, and let him try again after reviewing the particular element of the system which is being utilized in that chapter. If, after several trials he still has difficulty getting his meaning across to you (which is extremely unlikely) go on to the next phase of the work and come back to the problem at a later session. The elements have a cumulative effect and are arranged in such a manner that the farther along in the book the student progresses, the more clarity he will achieve concerning all previous elements.

It is well to begin each exercise session with a period of relaxation to lessen any muscular tension and prepare the child for his performance. The following methods have proven very satisfactory:

Limbering

Have the student stand easily, feet slightly apart, and *limber* his muscles by first rotating the head in a clockwise and then a counterclockwise direction, letting the chin drop loosely forward onto the chest and, as the head is rotated backwards, dropping the head as far to the back as it will go. Next, have him stretch out his arms and let them go limp, starting with the fingers, then hands, lower arms, upper arms, etc. Lifting each leg individually, while holding onto a chair for support, have him do the same with the legs, relaxing first toes, feet, then lower leg, upper, etc. Finally, have him bend the entire torso from the waist, letting it go limp as he describes a wide circle with the whole of his upper body.

The Stage Fall

It is important for anyone who is planning to appear onstage to learn to fall properly. If you will use the stage fall as an exercise in relaxation for your students, it will teach them to relax and at the same time give them practice for future roles in which they may have to portray a character who faints, is shot, or dies onstage:

Have the student stand naturally and concentrate first on his feet and ankles. He must think of his whole self as though he were melted butter or a huge raindrop. A fall never begins with the top of the body, but always with the feet and ankles. Have him direct his thought first to feet and ankles, letting them melt or drip until they collapse; then the lower legs, knees, upper legs, torso and the rest of the body will follow as a raindrop dripping down a windowpane. He should never reach out with arms or hands to protect himself. This is unnecessary and will stop the simple flow of the body downward. If the student thinks only of his complete fluidity and allows himself to gradually melt *downwards*, he will always fall gracefully and never hurt himself. Falling directly downward also minimizes the chance of striking furniture or other obstacles.

This technique can be used in real life, as well. The student about to trip or fall on the street, at school or at home should consciously relax, starting with the feet, and confidently let himself down. Thus he will avoid serious injury in any accidental fall. Try it yourself.

Since there are many restrictions in our lives, in these Exercises throughout the book we shall aim for as much freedom of action as possible. If the Exercises are being done at home, the parent must find an area in the house or apartment where the child (or children) may feel free to move about without the possibility of knocking over an expensive vase or other prized object. He needs a space large enough to move about in while giving expression to the thoughts, ideas and actions in each of the *Exercises*, and when performing his various *Practice Projects*. The teacher who uses this text in her classroom will generally have a cleared area at the front or back of the room where she and the pupils can work. If this is not feasible, perhaps the classes can be scheduled in the school auditorium during a free period, and the actual stage may be used for the *Exercises and Practice Projects*.

Parent/Teacher Guide: *Exercises and Practice Projects*

CHAPTER ONE

Exercise I: *Bodily Actions* (Page 3)

Have the pupil do these exercises in a cleared area, utilizing chairs or desks where necessary. Other props must be imagined. The pupil must make us "see" props by the way he "handles" them.

Practice Project (Page 5)

Parent: Listen to and/or watch the child's description/performance of the person he has chosen to study. See if it might be anyone you know.

Teacher: If your pupil is performing as another classmate and you work at these sessions with a group of students, have the others guess who the subject is — or guess yourself.

If there are any mannerisms or actions of the subject which you noticed the pupil left out in his performance, suggest he look further and repeat his performance next time.

CHAPTER TWO

Exercise II: *The Magic If* (Page 13)

Watch carefully as the student "handles" objects that are not there. Has he given you a sense of their weight and size? Has he made you see what he is holding? If not, have him go over the *Exercise* again, paying attention to this important aspect. If he cannot do it, give him an actual object (a ball, a book, a comb) to hold and then take it away and see if his *feeling memory* has improved. If it still has not — which is very unlikely — have him work on this at home before coming back to it at your next session.

Do not forget the element of humor. If the student turns one of these Exercises into a funny story, it should be done with as much attention to detail as it would be were it very serious. Do not allow the humor of his situation to blind you temporarily to the student's techniques. Enjoy it — but at the same time use your critical eye.

Practice Project (Page 16)

The student will not necessarily have to *stand* for this discussion of what he found on one block he normally passes through. It may be more comfortable for you to place a chair at the front of your working area and let him speak in conversational tones. If he does not remember too much, you should elicit information by questioning similar to that on page 16. Try to guess what street the child is describing (unless you come from another geographical area and do not spend much time in the vicinity of the school).

CHAPTER THREE
Exercise III: *Awareness and Imagination* (Page 25)
Parent/Teacher: Please do not be tempted to use another student to play the role of the tall

old man. We want here to build the child's imaginative and creative powers — so let him talk to an "air" man, but watch that he "sees" his antagonist and not just "air." If he does not at first "locate" the antagonist (in height and temperament), have him spend a few moments preparing by himself and then allow him to try again.

In the swimming pool Exercise watch for creation of atmosphere. Does the child really seem cold, wet and annoyed?

Practice Project (Page 26)

Does the semblance of old age come across in the child's portrayal? If not, talk it over with him to see if he actually saw an elderly person on whom to base his performance. Remind him to be specific, not general, in his creation.

Examine the play from which the child reads and be sure to listen carefully to the contrasts your student shows in his reading exercise. Has he found a way to alter the meaning of the text? To enhance it? Help him choose from among his approaches the one that seems correct for that character. Talk over the various approaches your student has found and explain why you feel the one chosen is right for the character and fits best in the context of the speech and the play.

CHAPTER FOUR

Exercise IV: *Concentration: Circles of Attention* (Page 33)

At the beginning of this session set up a "stage set" in your working area, with a focal point (perhaps chair and table with magazines, an ashtray, and a glass of water on it) and areas of lesser importance. (You might group a few chairs together farther off and put a stool or step-ladder beyond that. Use whatever you have at hand. The teacher may use movable desks or whatever she finds in the classroom.) These groupings then will represent the *circles of attention* and the student should be allowed to stand on the "stage" and direct his circles of attention gradually from small to medium to large (the whole stage area) as described.

Do not "strike the set" but allow the child to do this Exercise (particularly 3. and 4. with-in it) using objects (chairs, tables, and smaller objects) in the set itself as part of the Exercise. Bring to class, but do not let the student see beforehand, the items which you will use for

1. During this Exercise, use them as follows:

(a) A letter. Open the flap, pull the letter out of the envelope and unfold it.
(b) Turn the pages of a book.
(c) Snap open and then shut the top of your handbag.
(d) Open and shut a window, if there is one in the room. Otherwise use a door.
(e) Sweep the floor.
(f) Strike a match and then blow it out.
(g) Clap your hands together sharply.
(h) Open and shut your compact or your wallet. (If you use a wallet, remove some money and replace it.)

(i) Stir a spoon around in an empty cup.

[Add to the list yourself if you have time to do more — or choose any other objects you prefer.]

2. You should listen along with the child during a few minutes of "silence." When you say "time is up," and he begins enumerating what he has heard, check his list against what you yourself heard (what some of the others in the classroom heard).

3. When the child has replaced the object and has his back to you and it, you examine it as he tells you its properties. If he has not made too complete a list you may elicit more information by such questions as "How about its weight?" "Is it light or heavy?" "Is it really round or more oval in shape?"

4. Watch to see that the student spends enough time on each circle of attention really to concentrate within that circle before going on to the next. At the end of the *Exercise* ask him what he remembers about each and then you will be sure he has actually used all of his senses and not merely "looked" from one to the other.

Practice Project (Page 34)

Listen to the story the student tells about the object he has examined. Try to discover what it is, or (in school) have the class tell what it could be. If the story is not clear enough for identification, have the student enumerate all of the qualities or properties he found in the object. Then try again to identify it.

CHAPTER FIVE

Exercise V: The Senses(Page 40)

1. Prepare a tray of objects before class; be sure it is covered with a cloth or towel, so the student cannot see the items beforehand. These may be any household or school items — such as a spoon, napkin, box of matches, cup, glass, dish, pot, coaster, ruler, pencil, pen, small book, sheet of paper, ink bottle, eraser, labels, chalk — anything you can get together.

While the child examines them, you should be cataloguing their shape, color, size and qualities, so that when he describes them you can check for what he's missed.

2. Fill a paper bag with other objects (e.g., a washcloth, a sponge, a cake of soap, bottle of cologne or shaving lotion, pair of socks, baseball, tie, tie pin, ring, crayon, etc.) Keep the bag closed until time for this Exercise. Hand each one, in turn, to the student, giving him a few seconds to hold and examine it by touch.

3. Ask for quiet before you begin. Tear a sheet of paper. Write on the blackboard with chalk. Open the cap of a jar or bottle. Blow out an imaginary match. Pile several books one upon the other. Drop your shoe to the floor. Make the sound of a kiss. Open and shut a door or a window. Tap a pencil on the desk, against your teeth. Turn the light switch on and off.

(Add any sounds of your own choosing.)

4. Have ready on another covered tray several edible items, such as bread, a pickle, an apple, a cookie, a piece of candy, potato chips, dry cereal, raisins, nuts, vinegar, water (give the child a drop of the liquids on a spoon), segments of an orange or tangerine, spices such as

salt, sugar, pepper, nutmeg (Sprinkle a small amount of a spice into the child's palm, and let him touch his tongue to it.)

5. Have this group covered as well, so the student cannot tell beforehand what the items are. There is a wide range you may choose from: a jar of pickles, a bottle of cologne or shaving lotion, a piece of the orange, a bit of chocolate, a can of pepper, a box of bath powder, any of the foodstuffs previously used, a pouch of tobacco, a bottle of castor oil, wintergreen, caps from a cap pistol, any household product such as ammonia, liquid bleach, floor wax, furniture polish, a lump of clay, fresh flowers.

Practice Project (Page 40)

This time, because there is so much to work on, merely have the student repeat any of these sense developers for homework — particularly any he had difficulty with in class — having a friend or relative take the place of teacher or parent who prepares the objects and makes the sounds.

CHAPTER SIX
Exercise VI: The Action of the Voice (Page 48)

Wherever possible allow another student to fill roles such as the attendant in 1. and the mother in 2., etc. The parent should take these roles himself.

In these Exercises, check your reactions. Has the student shown different meanings for the same words? In the "age" Exercise, did you feel the age of the character?

Practice Project (Page 50)

Have the child tell you his ideas and methods for extending the senses. Each child should have an individual approach here. If he hasn't been too creative in his *Practice Project*, you may suggest methods which he can follow between now and the next session.

CHAPTER SEVEN

Exercise VII: *From Bodily Action to Inner Experience* (Page 58)

Let the student take enough time to work out these scenes in his mind before performing. For 5. you will have to be prepared. Before your class begins cut several pictures from magazines or newspapers. Choose a variety — such as an outdoor or landscape scene, photographs or portraits of individuals, action scenes, such as horse racing, stock car races, a police *stake-out* with all the men surrounding a *hideaway,* a peaceful pastoral or snowy mountain scene, etc. (If you can't find a good variety in magazines or newspapers, most larger libraries have classified picture collections from which you can borrow.)

Practice Project (Page 59)

In the *Practice Project* try to see and identify objects the child "handles." Listen to the student's memory experiences and be ready with your questions to bring out any colorful additions he may have left out. For instance, you may remind him in the *taste* memory discussion of all the other facets of that particular taste which he may have neglected or glossed over. This may add to his *sense* memory of that particular taste experience and it will help him use his taste memory better in the future.

CHAPTER EIGHT
Exercise VIII: *Truth on the Stage* (Page 68)

Do you see what the student is seeing? If he still sees the chair as a chair, so will you! If he should have any difficulty here, remove the chair for a moment and take its place. Now there is a person there. Have him see you and talk to you. Now replace the chair and have him "remember" you in its place. Now he will treat the chair as a specific person.

2. If you do not see the dancing partner, the dead pet, the sword in the child's improvised story, go back verbally with him for a moment and pick out the characteristics of each that will help him see. For example, is the dancing partner male or female? Tall, short, medium? Fat? Thin? Have him choose an actual person to visualize and then let him redo the *Exercise*.

3. Has the child differentiated sufficiently between the hot chocolate and the poison? If he "dies" after drinking the poison, watch his stage fall and be sure he relaxes completely, even though he may be having a "convulsion." The feet must go down first, the body following.

4. If at all possible, have the child leave the room until you have hidden the object. Do not use too large an object. When he searches the second time, watch for the suspense. If it isn't there, remind him that only his "watcher within" knows where it really is — the character he is portraying does not. In the rest of the *Exercises*, watch to see that all the actions are "truthful" so that you can see and identify all the "air" objects the student uses.

Practice Project (Page 69)

See last paragraph above. You may want to have a pitcher of water and a glass, an apple, etc., handy for use only in case the child needs a fresh reminder of the real thing before continuing without the actual object.

CHAPTER NINE

Exercise IX: *Actions and Reactions* (Page 80)

Teacher: Use other students for supporting roles in these Exercises. Parent: Take other roles yourself.

1. Does the child's performance bring out the full tragedy here? Do you care what happens? Has he projected his predicament? There need not be a second child in the scene but the student must *believe* he is there — must see him, hear him and *feel* his presence. He must react to the imaginary child's actions. As an experiment, you may do it both ways if you prefer — first with another student (or parent playing the role) and once more with only the memory of that person to help your student feel his presence.

2. You may also try this at an *actual* party, assigning the roles of secret agents and detectives to three children. Offer a prize if, at the end of the party, the "document" has been passed unnoticed.

3. and 4. How did the student handle his actions and reactions in these *Exercises*? If there were any areas that needed improvement, have him reread this chapter and do the *Exercise* again at home and repeat it at the next session.

Practice Project (Page 82)

Has the student learned from his observations at home? If he has only brushed the surface, create a scene where he can practice his observation *now*. You might use "shock value" by suddenly shouting at him; then have him tell you his immediate reaction to what just happened. Or you could simply get up and leave the room without a word. When you return, discuss his reaction to that action of yours. This creates spontaneity.

CHAPTER TEN

Exercise X (Page 90): *Action = What do I do?*
Aim or purpose = Why do I do it?
Adaptation or adjustment = How do I do it?

In this *Exercise*, check that the three elements are present in the student's work. Remember that even if his aim is *not achieved* — for example, in 1. she/he may not succeed in getting the dress/suit — that too is an adaptation or adjustment. Though his fictional purpose should fail, the *Exercise* may nevertheless be quite successful. See that the student has not forgotten any previous Stanislavski elements in any of the Exercises. While we are working here on adaptation, the other elements must be present as well. For example, in 5. his memory of feelings should come into play when he shows his reaction to the cold.

Practice Project (Page 99)

In the unlikely event he finds it difficult to merely talk about these personal adaptations, have him act out a particular instance for you or the class, and take the discussion from there.

CHAPTER ELEVEN

Exercise XI: *Speed and Beat or Tempo-Rhythm* (Page 98)

In these Exercises the student is not to act out the scene, but only to beat or tap it out, with the exception of 3. and 4. You will have to bring a radio, tape recorder or record player to class for 3. Choose records or tapes of varying tempos, or switch to different radio stations during the *Exercise* for a change of pace.

Practice Project (Page 99)

Examples from your own life may help draw out the particularly shy student. If you can tap out the different tempo-rhythms you experienced when you were rushing to get to a meeting, going to the supermarket, trying to get to the phone before it stopped ringing, sitting at a concert, etc., try to have him beat out these various rhythms along with you until he gets the idea and can show you his own.

CHAPTER TWELVE

Exercise XII: *Discovering Meaning Through Action* (Page 103)

Teacher: Have secondary roles played by other students. Parent: Take these roles yourself. Has the meaning shone through the actions in these four improvisations? If not, go over the text of Chapter Twelve with the student and let him try again. Lack of action is also considered an appropriate "action" in certain circumstances. For instance in 4. the student's character may be so frightened of the intruder that he is effectively immobilized. So he may be unable to do anything but hide.

Practice Project (Page 107)

It would be best if you read the play your student has chosen *before* this practice session. Discuss the play with the student class. Has he found the main aim? Has he coordinated his character's aim and actions with the play's aim? Are his choices of actions for his character logical within the context of the play?

Special Note to Teacher: When a play is chosen for a class performance, read it aloud in class before doing any work on the production. Discuss with the class the given circumstances of the play, as described by 1 through 10 on page101. As you assign the various roles, go over with each actor his character's aim in the play, and how the character serves to further the whole action of the play in achieving or failing to achieve his own aim within the given circumstances.

If you don't have time to do this in class, you might prepare a mimeographed sheet with a precis or shortened version of this information, to help the student organize his thinking as he prepares for the role.

CHAPTER THIRTEEN

Exercise XIII: *Super-Objective and Through Line of Action* (Page 112)

Teacher: Have other students portray the lions in the first Exercise, the monkeys in the second, etc. Parent: Since you cannot be *all* of these characters, it will be best to have the student use "air" characters — always making us see them as "real" through his actions and reactions and, of course his MAGIC IF. Do you feel the suspense in these Exercises? Has the student remembered all his previous Stanislavski elements?

Practice Project (Page 114)

Remembering the last *Practice Project*, discuss the story as if it were a play. Has the student found the main aim? Has he found true and logical *actions and counteractions* for his character in the given circumstances? You can use illustrations from the previous *Practice Project* to help him here.

CHAPTER FOURTEEN

Exercise XIV: *Posture and Speech* (Page 122)

Teacher: Use other students for supporting roles, including those of various animals. Parent: Take individual supporting roles yourself but have crowds (people at the state party, people on the breadline, etc.) imagined. Remind the student that they are there and he must "see" them if you are to see them. If he "bumps into" these non-existent people because he forgets their presence momentarily, work for awhile on creating individuals from the crowd. Describe several so he can picture them specifically for himself, and then he can use them in the scene. Has the student shown through his posture and speech, as well as his outer actions, what his inner actions are?

Practice Project (Page 123)

Have the student discuss at length his experience playing the role of his own parent. Did he learn anything new about his father/mother from this "costumed role?" Teacher: If you have not yet met the child's parent — would you "know" that parent anywhere from the child's parental observations here? Find out at the next PTA meeting or visiting night. Parent: It should be particularly interesting to you to discover the child's observations concerning yourself or your spouse. How do these jibe with your own?

CHAPTER FIFTEEN

Exercise XV: Creating Strange Characters (Page 131)

Watching your student perform as these "characters," you yourself will be stretching your imagination to greater limits. Here you must allow for fantasy. Do not expect ordinary characterizations. See how far the child can go in creative expression. Go along with him and be open to strange interpretations here. Try to "see" with the child's eyes.

Practice Project (Page 135)

Here is the final test. By now the teacher will know the child very well, although the parent, of course will have the advantage. Who could know this child better than you? Listen to this *Practice Project* closely to discover new things about your child which may help you to guide him even more efficiently in the future.

CHAPTER SIXTEEN: *More Work on the Part*(Page139)

There are no *Exercises* or *Practice Projects* in this last chapter. However, I suggest that both parent and teacher read this chapter aloud to the child/children. It sums up all of the previous work and therefore needs a session all to itself. After reading it, you and the child should discuss any factors you or he would like to review. If necessary, turn back to any previous chapter for a brief recapitulation. All the elements in the system have now been fused. The child is ready to begin.

Parent: Your work with your child will be its own reward. You may be looking forward to the time your child will appear onstage at school, church or in a local little theatre group. However, two tickets you might buy for the matinee performance of a professional play you and he can see together would provide a special and tangible inspiration for this moment of fulfillment. Directors and actors, after all, enjoy watching the work of their contemporaries . . . it adds a new perspective to their own.

Teacher: What a wonderful conclusion (to this work) it would be, to have the class play waiting in your drawer for just this moment! Now is the time to hand out the parts. Study is over. Work begins.

Now that the book is finished and both *actor* and *director* are ready to begin life onstage — I will close with the good luck epithet of theatre people everywhere: "Break a leg!"